ACTION-SEEKER
HANDBOOKS

JUNGLE
EXPLORER

MICHAEL COX

**Illustrated by
Stuart Holmes**

■ S C H

*Thanks to the staff of Nottingham City
and County Libraries*

Scholastic Children's Books
Commonwealth House, 1–19 New Oxford Street,
London, WC1A 1NU, UK
A division of Scholastic Ltd
London ~ New York ~ Toronto ~ Sydney ~ Auckland
Mexico City ~ New Delhi ~ Hong Kong

Published in the UK by Scholastic Ltd, 2004

Text copyright © Michael Cox, 2004
Illustrations copyright © Stuart Holmes, 2004
ISBN 0 439 97743 6

Introduction

To go into the jungle is to enter an awesome world: one that contains astonishing animals and mind-boggling plants, a world that is both mysterious, beautiful, inspiring and, in parts, extremely dangerous. It's a place that will fill you with wonder, astound you, and occasionally terrify you. And it will test your courage, intelligence, physical fitness, endurance and survival skills to their very limits.

Some action-seekers return to the jungle over and over again because they can't get enough of its never-ending variety of sights, sounds and sensations: screaming troops of howler monkeys, flocks of rainbow-coloured parakeets, towering waterfalls, graceful orang-utans, spiders the size of your fist, snakes as long as limousines, huge tropical storms that turn night into day, blistering heat and strange people, some of whom still live much as they did back in prehistoric times.

And the variety of jungles is endless. There's no such thing as a standard jungle. They range from the mangrove jungles of Asia with their swimming tigers, trees on stilts and eight-metre-long crocodiles, to the

Amazon jungle with its giant anaconda snakes, psychedelically coloured frogs and sky-scraping trees. You could spend a lifetime exploring the world's jungles and still only experience a fraction of their delights and wonders.

However, action-seeker, you can't just wander into these vast, uncharted terrains like you'd stroll into your local zoo or safari park. You have to be prepared, to know what you're doing, to be aware of the sort of extreme conditions you're going to have to endure, to know what clothing to wear, what equipment to take, and how to look after yourself should things take a turn for the worse (which they frequently do). Your Action-Seeker Handbook will tell you all of this and more. In it, you will discover how to cross a swollen jungle river without being swept to your doom; how to protect yourself from deadly snakes, insects and crocodiles should they attack; and how to live off the land when you suddenly find yourself without food and water. So what are you waiting for? If you're up to the jungle challenge, then this is the book for you. But take care, action-seeker, it's a jungle in here.

How to ...
get out and
about

PREPARING FOR YOUR JUNGLE ADVENTURE

There are a thousand reasons for exploring the jungle. You might be hoping to locate a lost tribe, check out some amazing wildlife, photograph tigers, or discover a weird insect that's yet to be named. Or maybe you want to test your courage, intelligence and physical prowess (or simply get away from tedious stuff like overdue homework, Sunday lunch with the rellies and bedroom-tidying reminders). Whatever the reason for your adventure, action-seeker, it's essential that you're properly prepared. The moment you embark on your jungle trek you'll leave the 21st century behind and enter a place that is much the same as it was a thousand years ago. All evidence of modern technology will vanish in an instant. There will be no cars, roads, hospitals, shops, police stations, or any of the other convenient and reassuring things we take for granted, so you will have to be totally self sufficient. And that means making meticulous and painstaking preparation before you set off.

1 Get yourself fit. Walking through the jungle is really tiring, especially if the vegetation is extra thick or there are hills to climb. You may well have to hack your way through dense foliage for hour after hour. If you're not in peak condition, this will leave you aching, breathless and drenched in sweat in no time (especially if you've run out of tropical-strength underarm deodorant).

2 Get acclimatized (i.e. get used to the conditions). It will take you a few days, maybe even a few weeks, to feel reasonably comfortable in the hot, damp atmosphere of the rainforest.

The loud noises of the birds and monkeys, the non-stop buzzing insects, the amazing, huge trees and plants will also take quite a bit of getting used to.

In preparation for your expedition, try taking short strolls in there to start with. Or, if you don't happen to have a small friendly jungle near you, just spend a few days walking in circles at your local sauna, greenhouse dealer, garden centre or zoo.

3 Find out about the dangerous plants and animals you're likely to meet so you know what to expect and what you must do if they turn nasty. Look at unlabelled pictures of jungle creatures and plants and see how quickly you can identify them. Try these for a start:

Is this...
a) A leech.
b) A lychee.
c) A sausage.

Is this...
a) A fire ant.
b) A fire engine.
c) An anaconda.

4 Practise swimming. Because much of the jungle is impossible to walk through, you may well do a lot of travelling by river on some sort of boat, such as a canoe or a raft with an outboard motor. And there's always the chance that you will be capsized by some mishap e.g. when a crocodile or hippo upends your boat (or your guide decides to treat you to his Elvis impersonation). So being able to swim well could save your life.

5 Get clued up on all the places you're going to visit. Learn about the most important features of the landscape from maps, guide books and charts. Stuff like the positions and names of the main rivers, the most dangerous swamps, any awkward hilly areas (and the handiest burger bars and Internet cafes).

6 Learn about the people who live in the area of jungle you're going to explore. Learn a few words of their language so you can say things like:

Hello!

Goodbye!

Oh dear I appear to have lost my tent/way/ passport/ canoe/clothes /marbles!

And make sure you learn some of their customs. It's no good greeting a powerful jungle tribal chieftain by grinning at him and vigorously shaking his hand when, in his culture, a grin means that you think he is a worthless lump of parrot poo and a handshake means that you're intending to barbecue his children and serve them up to him on a banana leaf. That sort of thing's just asking for trouble. And it's really important that you get to be pals with these people and win their affection and confidence because one day you may be depending on their help, local knowledge, goodwill (and mobile phones) for your survival. They can also help you by giving you the benefit of their traditional wisdom, like showing you the safest spot to cross a river, the sort of places to avoid because they're infested with piranhas, what plants you can and can't eat (and the best sort of ant to serve with boiled monkey livers).

7 Leave a travel plan with someone you can trust so that: **a)** they can tell rescuers where to begin looking for you if you don't return on time; and **b)** they can make good use of your football season ticket if you're gone for ever.

8 And finally, before setting out on your action-seeking adventure, you must read some sort of jungle exploration handbook, packed full of essential survival and travel tips plus fascinating facts and stories – but then you're doing that already!

YOUR CLOTHING AND EQUIPMENT

There's no point in setting off on your jungle trek dressed and equipped as if you're about to enjoy a day at the beach or go on a countryside ramble. Being properly kitted out will make the difference between your adventure being a dismal disaster or a rip-roaring success.

Lightweight long trousers, long-sleeved shirt and jacket
All made from strong 'rip-stop' cotton which won't be easily torn by thorns and spikes. You should have two sets of clothes, one to wear during the day, which will remain permanently wet from the jungle dampness and your sweat, and a dry set to wear during the night.

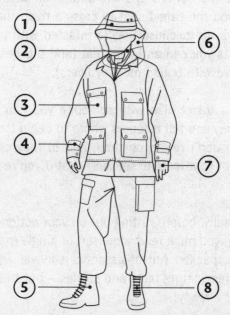

① *Wide-brimmed hat keeps off rain and sun, protects you from some insects (and makes you look like Crocodile Dundee).*

② *Collar can be raised to protect your neck.*

③ *Large pockets to hold big items of equipment in, e.g. your canoe.*

④ *Wristbands (soaked in insect repellent).*

⑤ *Ankle-high jungle boots made from rubber and synthetic nylon or Gore-Tex.*

⑥ *Mosquito head-net protects your face – just fold it and pop it in your pocket when you don't need it (the hat, not your face).*

⑦ *Gloves to protect your hands from thorns, blisters and wait-a-whiles (see page 27).*

⑧ *Boot laces made from parachute cord to stop them rotting in the jungle dampness.*

Neck cord and attachments

Tuck them all inside your shirt when you're trekking.

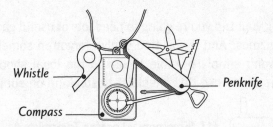

Whistle

Penknife

Compass

Belt and attachments

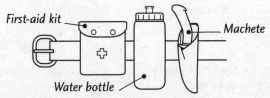

First-aid kit

Machete

Water bottle

A word about jungle rot

Many action-seeking jungle explorers don't wear any undies. Why? Well, when you've had a good soaking from a tropical downpour your undies will stay wet for yonks. And do you remember how it felt toddling around in those yukky wet nappies when you were aged 18 months? Yes, absolutely horrible! And it's the same in the jungle because your wet undies won't dry anywhere near as speedily as your outies. As a result, they may cause 'chaffing' as you walk and that could well lead to you getting the horrid itchy condition known as 'jungle rot'. And if jungle rot affects you in the Congo basin area it could completely ruin your expedition (not to mention your Congo basin area).

GETTING PROPERLY KITTED OUT

During your trip you're going to need lots of useful gadgets and gizmos. And if you find you've forgotten something you won't simply be able to nip to the local shop and pick it up, so use this checklist to stock up on supplies:

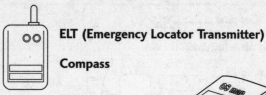

ELT (Emergency Locator Transmitter)

Compass

Maps
Preferably for the bit of jungle you're intending to visit.

Medical kit:
Anti-malaria tablets
Antihistamine tablets – for insect
bites (just in case you meet any
badly bitten insects)
Antiseptic ointment and plasters –
for scratches and cuts
Insect repellent – jungle strength!
(NB it doesn't just repel ants).

Machete and a sharpening stone
A really important bit of kit.

Pen knife
With lots of foldaway blades.

Collapsible water bottle
5-litre size.

Fish hooks and line

Action-Seeker Tip

Bring along some small but useful things to swap or give as
presents in case you meet any local jungle people. Knives,
scissors, fish hooks and fishing line, bottles of aspirin, baseball
caps, school equipment (as well as luxury fitted kitchens and
top-of-the-range sports cars) will all be much appreciated.

Camera and films
You'll want to record your adventures and will kick yourself if you don't.

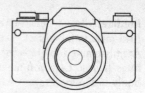

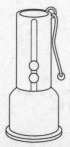

Waterproof torch and batteries

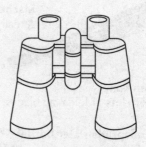

Binoculars
For checking out birds, treetop flowers, monkeys etc.

Signal mirror

Whistle

Sunglasses
For river travel – the glare from the water can be fierce.

Parachute cord (15 metres)
For rigging up shelters, washing
lines (or volley ball courts).

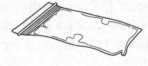

**Mosquito
netting**

Lighter

Resealable plastic bags
To protect things from the jungle dampness.

Backpack
To keep all your kit in.

A word about tents

A lot of action-seekers aren't too keen on taking tents on
jungle adventures because...

a) They're heavy to carry along with all that other
equipment – after a day's trekking even light loads can
feel like they weigh a ton!

b) If you forget to zip up your tent flaps when you go to
bed there's the possibility that all sorts of creepy-crawlies,
such as snakes and scorpions, will sneak in during the
night and snuggle up to you.

So, rather than taking a tent on your trip, you might find it far more rewarding to make your own jungle shelter (see page 60). However, you will need to take a hammock. The native Indians of South America invented hammocks. They're ideal for jungle expeditions because they keep you off the ground away from creepy-crawlies.

Food to take

You'll be able to find food and water in the jungle without too much difficulty (see pages 80–103). Nevertheless, it's a good idea to take along some basic rations to fall back on if the going gets tough.

Action-Seeker Tip

Tinned food is quite heavy to carry so many action-seekers take lightweight, dehydrated (dried) food on their treks and add water to it when they're ready to eat it.

Flavourings and mixers

When you're using food you get from the wild it's a good idea to add some spices and flavourings to give it a bit of zip and zest. Salt is essential as you will be sweating so much. Without replacing lost salt you will suffer cramps. Also take things like sugar and flour to combine with the things you get from nature.

Suggested daily rations

Breakfast: Breakfast is really important for giving you the energy to tackle challenges ahead. Dried fruits, muesli or oats will all set you up for an action-packed day.

Trail snacks: A good way to keep up your energy while you're trekking and to stave off hunger pangs until you get your main meal is to nibble things like biscuits, crackers and cereal bars.

Main meals: As a treat you could prepare a tasty dehydrated meal such as beef stroganoff and noodles, mashed potatoes and roast turkey (or settle for the usual curried orang-utan).

WARNING

Don't be tempted to eat your dehydrated food before it's soaked up the necessary amount of water, otherwise it will absorb water from your body. Combined with the huge amount of body fluids you lose through sweating you'll end up in trouble (i.e. one third action-seeker, two thirds digestive biscuit).

HAVE YOU BEEN PAYING ATTENTION?

1 The best way to prepare for your jungle expedition is to ...
a) watch loads of old Tarzan movies.
b) get really fit.
c) go to the local zoo and wrestle crocodiles.

2 In order to avoid the body fungus known as jungle rot, many explorers walk through the rainforest ...
a) in huge fluffy nappies.
b) completely starkers.
c) minus their underwear.

3 It's a good idea to soak your wristbands in ...
a) insect repellent.
b) the Indian Ocean.
c) treacle.

4 Many action-seekers aren't keen on tents because ...
a) they're forever forgetting to zip up their flies.
b) tents are heavy to carry.
c) they scared of being arrested for 'loitering within tent'.

5 The best sort of food to take on a jungle expedition is ...

a) oodles of hot custard, jam roly-poly and spotted dick.

b) dehydrated food and energy-giving snacks.

c) crate-loads of bananas and coconuts.

SETTING OFF ON THE JUNGLE TRAIL

So, action-seeker, now you're all kitted up and ready to go. A jeep has taken you to the point where your jungle trail begins, but now the road has run out and it's time to strike out on your own. If, like so many other action-seekers before you, you have chosen to explore a lowland rainforest, such as those you find in the Amazon and Congo basins, Indonesia, Australasia and the Pacific Islands, the main sort of terrain you'll encounter will be 'primary' jungle, which is fairly easy to trek through. So, when you travel through it, you'll be able to spend time enjoying the awesome new sights and sounds that will greet your eyes and ears at every turn. However, it won't entirely be a leisurely stroll through the park. You'll have to be alert and jungle-wise. And you'll definitely need to take precautions to avoid creepy-crawlies and prevent yourself from getting lost. Let's get going...

Moving through primary jungle

1 Carry a stick and use it to part the vegetation as you walk. Your stick will also help to knock ants, spiders and snakes from leaves, stems and branches and consequently they will be less likely to bite you.

2 Stop every now and again to listen and check your map and your position (see page 40). You might hear the sound of nearby water, indicating you're almost at that river or waterfall you may well have been heading for. (If you hear the sound of Big Ben chiming, on the other hand, it means that your map is completely rubbish.)

Action-Seeker Tip

Always have a full water bottle with you. Drink at least half a litre every hour while you're trekking and a quarter of a litre every other hour while you're resting.

3 If you're going up a steep slope, move in a zig-zag pattern so that you tackle the gradient bit by bit. You'll find it less tiring. Don't be tempted to grab bushes or vines to give yourself a pull up. They may be covered in sharp spines and thorns (or a thick coating of fresh gorilla poo).

WARNING

As you move forward don't pull on vines if you cannot see what they are attached to. You may end up bringing a dead branch or tree crashing down on top of you.

4 Avoid dangerous obstacles such as swamps and steep drops.

5 Occasionally stop and stoop down to look at the jungle floor. You may spot an animal trail that you can follow (or some ten-pound notes dropped by previous explorers).

MEETING THE JUNGLE CHALLENGE

You've just got the hang of trekking through primary jungle, but suddenly you find the going much more difficult. You're surrounded by a mass of vegetation. Vines and creepers attempt to trip you up or strangle you at every step. Sharp thorns rip at your clothes and skin, while thousands of biting insects do their best to make a meal of you. The intense damp heat is mind-numbing and you're deafened by the shriek of parrots and the buzz and whirr of insects. Then you look at your watch and realize that in the last hour you haven't travelled more than three or four metres!

Action-seeker, what you've entered is a patch of

'secondary' jungle! This is jungle which has been cleared and cultivated by local people but later abandoned, allowing a huge tangle of trees, bushes and creepers to grow again. But don't despair, there are techniques for dealing with secondary jungle and you'll soon learn to move through the thick undergrowth like an expert.

1 Move through the jungle smoothly, not like a hippo in a PC shop, but sort of 'wiggle' as you walk. In other words, shorten or lengthen your stride so that you slide between the undergrowth. Shift your hips, turn your shoulders, bend your body (and twitch your funky butt to that crazy jungle beat, daddio!).

Action-Seeker Tip

Take extra care when you're around tall jungle grasses. Some are so sharp they will cut you like knives.

2 Develop 'jungle eye'. This is not some horrible tropical disease but the ability to: **a)** ignore the bushes and trees which are immediately in front of you; and **b)** focus on the more distant jungle, looking for natural breaks in the foliage through which you can pass. In other words look *through* the jungle, not at it.

3 Use your machete to cut your way through dense vegetation. But...
a) Don't get carried away and attempt to cut down the entire jungle as this will leave you feeling very tired.
b) Cut *upwards* when you're cutting vines. Sound carries long distances in the jungle and this way of hacking reduces noise.
c) Avoid mistaking your own leg for a tree branch – this could lead to quite a lot of pain and discomfort. And more to the point, attempting to hop through an entire rainforest on just one leg could be very tiring.

Action-Seeker Tip

If you feel faint, light-headed or sick, sit down in the shade, drink something cool and pour some water over yourself. Also try wafting yourself with a fan (but only if you happen to have brought along an adoring admirer with you).

4 If you can skirt round an obstacle like a hill or an area of extra-dense jungle, do so. To make a detour is far less tiring than climbing slopes or hacking at vegetation in the exhausting tropical heat and humidity.

Jungle tale

A group of airmen crashed in the jungle. As they set off in search of help and civilization they found their way blocked by an area of dense bamboo forest. It took them five days to hack their way through it. They later discovered that they could have circled around it in about four hours.

Escaping from the wait-a-while vine

You're moving forward quite well now but all of a sudden you find yourself gripped by an unseen force. You try to move on but you can't. So you decide to go sideways. But you can't do that either! You look down and see that the thorns of a large plant have hooked themselves into your clothes and, despite your efforts, it seems to have you trapped! Action-seeker, you've walked straight into the clutches of what is known as the wait-a-while vine. It has incredibly sharp and painful spikes that will rip through both your clothes and flesh. If you get hooked up in it you could be stuck for ages (which is how it gets its name), possibly for days! Here's how to escape from this horrible predicament: Stay calm and remain completely still. If you've got a pal with you, ask them to untangle you. If you're on your own, slowly and carefully *reverse* the process by which you became entangled. Gradually move backwards carefully unhooking the spikes from your togs and flesh as you do.

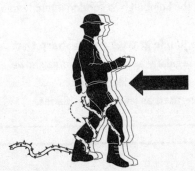

HAVE YOU BEEN PAYING ATTENTION?

1 The best way to move through the jungle is ...
a) backwards.
b) smoothly.
c) in an air-conditioned limousine.

2 When you're moving through primary jungle always carry ...
a) on like someone who's not quite right-in-the-head.
b) a large sign saying 'eat my shorts'.
c) a stick to part vegetation.

3 If you pull on a jungle vine you could ...
a) bring a dead tree crashing down.
b) flush every loo in Rio de Janeiro.
c) bring the Edinburgh to London Intercity to a dead stop.

4 Some jungle grasses are so sharp that ...
a) they regularly appear on TV quiz shows.
b) they can cut you like a knife.
c) they're used as lawn-mower blades.

CROSSING WATER

As you travel through the jungle, action-seeker, you're going to have to cross large expanses of water, usually in the form of swamps or rivers. And knowing the correct way to do this is absolutely crucial to your survival!

You've been for a day's trek through the jungle to explore some ancient ruins. On your journey out you splashed across a shallow stream that was no more than a trickle. However, the daily afternoon downpour which occurs in many lowland rainforest jungles was about six times heavier than usual, so you return to find that the trickle has become a muddy torrent which now blocks your way back to camp. You're unsure about entering the fast-flowing water but it'll be dark in 20 minutes and the river's getting deeper as each minute passes. You also sense that some of the more dangerous creatures of the jungle are about to begin their nightly hunt for prey! It looks like you've no choice but to cross the river. Here's what to do:

1 Carefully identify the best spots to enter and exit the water:

a) Avoid steep slopes or rocky banks.

b) Enter the river on the straighter stretches between the bends. Water flows fastest on the outside of bends.

c) Choose firm ground where there is no mud which could trap you by sucking your feet down the moment you enter it.

d) Steer clear of debris, vegetation or fallen trees which could affect your progress or drag you under as they're swept against you by the current.

Action-Seeker Tip

Never cross a river with your rucksack fully strapped to your back. If it becomes waterlogged it could trap you beneath the water. Instead, sling it over the shoulder which will be facing downstream. Then, if the current catches you, it won't push you and the rucksack over or drag you both along, it'll just pull it off your shoulder.

2 Keep your boots on; they'll provide a better grip.

3 If you're not already carrying one, cut a long pole from a tree and use it to test the depth of the water.

4 Enter the water by lowering yourself in – don't jump into it.

Action-Seeker Tip

Watch out for marks on the bank that look as if someone's dragged a big log through it. Especially if there are lizard-like footprints with it. It means there'll more than likely be crocodiles in the water.

5 Be prepared for deep mud, sudden changes in water depth and underwater plants that may wrap around your legs and feet.

6 When you start crossing, face upstream so that: **a)** the water pushes your legs back, locking them at the knees; and **b)** you can spot any dangerous objects the current is carrying towards you and get out of their way.

7 Use the pole and your feet to create a triangle shape (for stability), then move one foot at a time but don't walk in the way you normally would on a pavement. Follow this sequence:
a) Move the pole first – to test the river bed.
b) Press on the pole and move your right leg.
c) Press on the pole and move your left leg.
   Keep repeating the sequence (though once you reach the opposite bank you may stop if you wish).

Building a raft

If you find that the water you need to cross is too deep to wade through safely, you will need to build a raft.

1 To make your raft deck, use your machete to cut ten strong logs of roughly equal length. They should be long enough to carry you, your equipment and your companions (plus a couple of dozen enormous hairy sailors).

2 Cut four more logs, each a little longer than the width of the deck. You'll use these to make the retaining frames that will go at each end of your raft.

3 Using your machete, cut notches along the length of each of your retaining logs. Don't make the notches too deep or you'll weaken the frame.

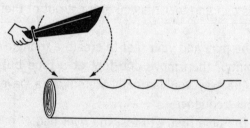

4 Lie the deck logs on the notches of the lower retaining logs, keeping them as level as possible. It's important that they all fit together really snugly (logs have feelings too, you know).

5 Place the upper retaining logs on the section of deck above the lower retaining logs.

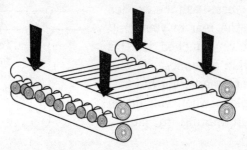

6 Using ropes, lash the upper and lower retaining logs of your raft together at each corner as tightly as you can to make the raft really solid and stable. Use reef knots (see page 67) to secure the ropes.

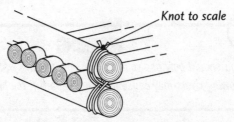

Knot to scale

If there's time, you can also lash the individual logs to the frame along the entire width of the raft.

Action-Seeker Tip

Keep the knots uppermost so that you can check them and tighten them if necessary when your raft is in the water.

7 Lash two short branches together to make a small wooden cross. Lash the wooden cross to the rear of your craft after you've launched it. This will provide a support for your paddle (or a marker for your last resting place when you drown whilst attempting to launch your raft).

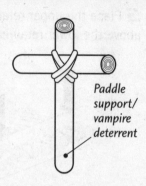

Paddle support/ vampire deterrent

8 Well done, action-seeker, your raft is now complete. Why not name it? Maybe something like Jungle Queen, Amazon Conqueror (or Titanic II).

WARNING

You should only use your raft on slow-flowing water as faster-flowing rivers may cause it to come apart at the seams!

Making a paddle
Before setting off on your raft, it's important to make a paddle.

1 Use your machete to strip and taper a strong green branch to a wedge-shaped ending.

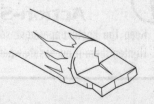

2 Lash two short straight pieces of wood on either side of the wedge.

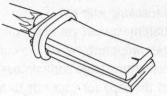

3 Jam a third piece of wood between the two short pieces and make it secure.

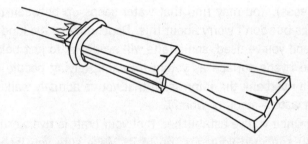

You will use your paddle to propel your raft and to steer it by supporting it on the wooden cross and moving it to the left (if you want to go right) and to the right (if you wish to go left). Remember that (unlike jet skis and power boats) rafts turn quite slowly, so make allowances for this when you're steering.

Action-Seeker Tip

If you want to stand up while you're steering, lash a long branch to the handle of your paddle. This will give you more reach (and will also come in handy for walloping passing crocodiles).

Launching your raft

Before you put your raft in the water, make sure it won't get swept away when the current catches it by tying it to something large and immovable. Leave enough slackness in the rope for your raft to move about a bit so you can properly test its strength, stability and buoyancy.

Launch your raft by lifting up one side with poles. It should then slide smoothly into the water (or fall to pieces). You may find that water seeps up between the logs but don't worry about this. Depending on the kind of wood you've used, some rafts will even sink to just below the river's surface as you're travelling (giving people on the riverbank the impression that you're actually walking on water – cool, or what?).

Once you've established that your craft is riverworthy, you can load your gear on to it. Make sure you lash it down to make it secure.

Swamp tactics

You're making your way through a particularly boggy area of jungle when you suddenly find that your feet are being sucked into the ground. Too late, you realize that you've entered a deep jungle swamp and are now rapidly sinking into the ooze that is hidden beneath the vegetation. The pull of the mud on your feet is overwhelming and irresistible. You begin to struggle against the sucking mud but the more you thrash about, the deeper you sink. The gloop is soon up to your chin.

In a few more minutes it will cover your mouth and nose!
A horrible end is looming ... but it needn't be that way,
action-seeker. Here's what to do if you're unlucky
enough to fall into a swamp: If you find yourself sinking
really quickly, take off your rucksack. It will hinder your
escape efforts and you may well be able to hook it out
of the swamp later on. Do not panic and do not struggle.
This will only make your situation worse. Now fall onto
your back and spread your arms and legs. This will help
you to float on the surface of the swamp, like you would
in a swimming pool. Then, using a sculling stroke, swim
until you reach firm ground. Sorted!

Technique for swamp escape
(bog-standard method)

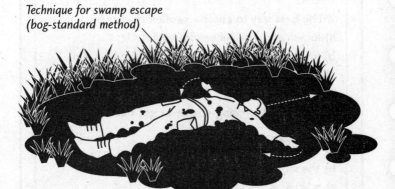

Action-Seeker Tip

If the swamp has tussocks of grass growing from it, you may be
able to run across it, using the tussocks as stepping stones.

HAVE YOU BEEN PAYING ATTENTION?

1 If the mud at the edge of a river looks as if it's had a big log pulled through it, it means that you're likely to meet ...
a) some people pulling big logs.
b) crocodiles.
c) a sticky end.

2 The best way to enter a swollen river is by ...
a) lowering yourself in very carefully.
b) a triple somersault with a quarter-turn back-flip.
c) diving from the top of the tallest tree you can find.

3 The best swimming stroke to get out of a swamp with is ...
a) the butterfly.
b) the moth.
c) a 'sculling' backstroke.

How to ...
avoid getting
lost

GETTING YOUR BEARINGS

Getting lost in the jungle is an easy thing to do! There are no real paths, no signposts, it's huge and green all over, and one bit looks just like any other. And because some types of rainforest are so incredibly dense and tangled, you can soon feel like you've shrunk to the size of an ant and have become trapped inside a sort of vast and never-ending green nightmare which you'll never escape from. However, there are ways to navigate your way around the jungle. And the most basic of them is direction-finding.

Using your compass

Imagine you've been out on a firewood-gathering expedition but have become slightly disorientated during your search for fuel. You know that your camp is only a 20-minute walk to the north of where you are now but you no longer know which way is north. Then you remember that you have a compass in your pocket. All you have to do now is use it to discover which way is north.

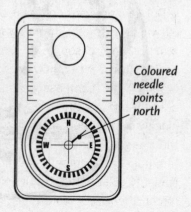

Coloured needle points north

1 Place your compass on your open palm (that's the palm of your hand, not a coconut palm).

2 Turn the compass slowly around.

3 You should now notice that the coloured end of the needle (normally red) always points in the same direction. That direction is north.

Things to remember about your compass

● Make sure you always hold your compass flat. If you don't, the needle will touch the bottom or top of the housing (compass holder) and then it won't always point to the north.

● Try not to hold it near any magnets or metal objects or the red arrow will be attracted to them and will no longer accurately indicate where north is.

● Don't watch your compass constantly. You may ending up walking straight into a swamp (or a crocodile's jaws).

● If for any reason (e.g. profound stupidity; believing you've turned into a howler monkey) you can't recall the order of the compass points, remember that: **a)** the points start at the top; and **b)** they go around in a clockwise direction. Then, as you hack your way through the jungle, constantly repeat one of the following reminders to yourself: Never Eat Shredded Wheat or Naughty Elephants Squirt Water and you will never forget them. (Or you'll be mistaken for a wandering forest spirit by the local people.)

Blazing a trail

Another useful and sure-fire way of finding your way back to your jungle camp is by blazing a trail. You simply mark trees in the four different compass directions that lead to your camp. Here's how to mark the trees. Make two *small* cuts in each tree on the side of the trunk facing your camp. These are your return route markers. Make one *large* cut on the side of the tree trunk which faces away from your camp. These are your outward route markers. So even if you are finding your way back to camp in the dark you shouldn't have a problem. You simply feel the tree trunks to work out which way to go.

Coping with getting separated from your party

You're wandering through the jungle with your pals, marvelling at the rainbow-coloured tree frogs and listening to giant hornbills screeching in the branches above you.

Suddenly, just as you get to a point where the trail forks in three directions, you notice a huge beetle sitting on a plant leaf. You stop to admire its brilliant red-and-gold markings and its antennae, each of which must be at least three centimetres long. You take out your camera and take four or five snaps of the incredible creature. Then you turn to your companions to tell them about it. But, as you do, you see nothing but green ... green ... and more green, but no human beings whatsoever.

The truth hits you like a punch in the stomach. Your pals have wandered on without you. And more to the point, you've no idea which trail they've taken. All you know is that suddenly you're on your own in an area of jungle the size of Belgium. And all you have with you is your knife, a small water bottle (which is almost empty) and a few other odds and ends.

Your mouth goes dry. Sharp pains of anxiety grip your fevered brain. You've *got* to find your pals! First you dash down one trail. But there's no sign of them. So you rush back and try another trail. And then you give up on that one. You now try to find the point at which you stopped to take the photograph. But you aren't sure where that is any more. All the time you cry out your friends' names in a voice made faint with terror but you know that with each second that ticks away you are probably becoming more and more isolated from them. Even if they return to see what's happened to you there's little chance they'll find you. It's only an hour or so until nightfall. What are you to do?

1 Don't panic. Stay very calm. Remember the word STOP (Sit – Think – Observe – Plan). Don't run around like a headless chicken and make a bad situation worse!

2 Make lots of noise. This may attract the attention of your companions and enable them to locate you.

3 If you don't relocate your party immediately, choose a direction and keep walking until you get to a stream. Make sure you use a compass bearing (see page 40), otherwise you could end up going round in circles. Also leave obvious signs that you've headed that way using your machete. Follow the water downstream until you reach a big river then follow that downstream too. Most jungle people live near rivers and use them for transport, so you should meet helpful humans sooner or later. As you travel...

a) Look for signs of man-made structures.

b) If you have a whistle, blast it every now and again; if not, just yell.

c) Carefully use your knife to mark your trail so that you can find your way back to the spot you started from (see page 42).

Action-Seeker Tip

Don't forget to rest and eat as you attempt to find your way. If you're tired, hungry and too hot or too cold you will make mistakes. And if you make mistakes you are more likely to perish!

Finding your way using a stick

You're out on a trek, but have been so busy following some howler monkeys which have been swinging through the trees above you that you've completely forgotten to carry out regular map and compass checks. Nor have you bothered to keep a note of which trails you've been following. You've no idea where you are, but you do know that your camp lies directly to the west of you. You reach into your pocket for your trusty compass. It's no longer there. You've lost it! As you realize that your compass is now more than likely being used as a traffic island by the local insect population, your heart sinks to your boots. It's vital that you discover which way is west. Your life depends on it! Here's what to do:

1 Get a straight stick, about one metre long (available from all good stick outlets, i.e. 'trees').

2 Take your stick to a level bit of ground where there are few plants growing.

3 Stick your stick in the ground. If the sun is shining your stick will cast a shadow on the ground.

Don't give up on this technique – stick at it

4 Mark the tip of the shadow tip with a stone or a twig. This first shadow mark will be west. It's always west, everywhere on earth. Honest!

5 Now wash your hands (they're probably a bit *sticky!*).

Finding your way using the sun and shadows

As you spend more and more time in the wild you will soon become expert at using shadows to discover what time it is and to find directions. Here are a few handy pointers:

● The sun always rises more or less in the east and sets more or less in the west. So if you climb out of your sleeping bag in the morning and look at the sun you can be sure that the direction you are looking in is east.

● In the northern half of the world, the sun will be due south of you when it's at its highest point in the sky which is usually around lunchtime.

● In the southern half of the world, this same noonday sun will mark due north.

● When the sun is at its highest point in the sky, objects cast hardly any shadows.

● In the northern half of the world, shadows move in a clockwise direction.

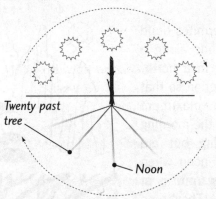

Twenty past tree

Noon

● In the southern half of the world, shadows move in an anti-clockwise direction.

Finding your way using the moon

● The moonlight you see is a reflection of the sun's rays. The moon has no light of its own (and is made of green cheese). As the moon moves from out of the earth's shadow, it begins to reflect light from its right side.

- If the moon rises before the sun has set, the shiny side will be the west.
- If the moon rises after midnight, the shiny side will be the east.
- If you're travelling at night this knowledge will give you a rough idea of where east and west are.

Finding your way using other natural direction indicators

- Some termites build their mounds along a line going in a north-south direction so that they get maximum warmth in the morning and evening but are shaded at noon when the sun's warmth is at its hottest. (They're no fools, those termites.)

- Certain sorts of weaver birds only build their nests on the west-facing sides of trees.
- Plants always grow towards the sun, so in the northern half of the world they tend to face south and in the southern half of the world they face north.

SIGNALLING FOR HELP

You may well get into a situation in the jungle where you need to be got out really quickly. For instance, if you're completely and utterly lost! Or if one of your party is bitten by a snake (or suddenly remembers they've forgotten to cancel their milk). To do this you must use signals to attract attention to your position. Here are some ways to do it:

● Use your torch. To send an SOS signal, press down the switch quickly three times in succession to make three short flashes followed by three long flashes, followed by three short flashes. That stands for SOS (Save Our Souls).

● Send your message using the Ground-to-Air Emergency Code. You can do this by 'writing' it out in a clearing using clothing or cutting the message out of the jungle vegetation. Here are the symbols you must use:

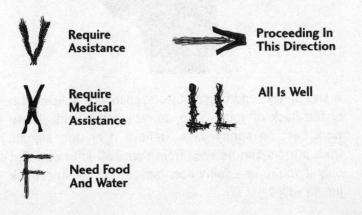

Require Assistance

Proceeding In This Direction

Require Medical Assistance

All Is Well

Need Food And Water

• Use body signals to say what you need:

a) Both arms raised with palms open means 'I need help'.

b) One arm raised with palm open means 'I do not need help'. (Or 'Hmm, it's started raining again'.)

• Use mirrors and bright objects, such as a polished tin or the back of your watch, to reflect the light. These work best on sunny days. Believe it or not, signals from mirrors can be seen from over 130 km away. But only if you're in a fairly open space and not in a thick jungle valley.

Action-Seeker Tip

Remember, almost any signal repeated three times is usually recognized as a distress signal.

● Tie a flag or brightly coloured cloth to a pole and wave it in a figure-of-eight pattern.

● Use fire. Find a big clearing in the jungle and build three fires to make a triangle shape. The triangle is an international distress symbol. You can also burn a tree to attract attention. This works best when it's dark (of course!).

Action-Seeker Tip

During daylight hours put lots of damp or green vegetation on your fire to create white smoke that will contrast against the green foliage.

● Use your clothing. Spread it on the ground or on top of a tree (not all of it though, or you may find yourself feeling pretty embarrassed if your rescuers turn up really quickly). Use your most brightly coloured clothes, as they're more likely to be seen. Set the clothes out in an unnatural-looking geometrical pattern so that someone passing overhead doesn't mistake them for a tropical plant (or a giant lizard on its way to a disco).

If your signal is spotted and understood by an aircraft during daylight or moonlight, the pilot will rock the aircraft from side to side. At night they'll make green flashes with the plane's signal lamp. If your signal is spotted but not understood, the aircraft will make a complete circle (during day or moonlight) or will make red flashes with its signal lamp (at night). If this happens you must make your signals more clear (or learn your alphabet).

Jungle tale

Four American soldiers became lost in the jungle on an island in the Pacific Ocean. They decided to stay put in the clearing they found themselves in, in the hope that a search party would use their last reported position to come and find them. After a while they began to worry that the search party might miss them. Then they suddenly got the idea of whistling to attract attention, so they cut down bamboo stems and made them into flutes. To start with they took turns to constantly whistle the SOS signal: three short blasts, followed by three long ones, followed by three more short ones. Nothing much happened so after a while all four of them decided to blow their flutes together so that the louder sound might carry further. At that moment the rescue party were just about to pass the clearing which was hidden from them by a dense bamboo grove. Alerted by the shrill sounds of the flutes, they found the men and got them safely back to base. Had they not heard the flutes they might well have passed the clearing and ended up searching miles away from the lost soldiers.

HAVE YOU BEEN PAYING ATTENTION?

1 The best way to attract attention to yourself is …
a) by saying something really outrageous.
b) by lighting three signal fires.
c) by running around with your underpants on your head.

2 The ground-to-air 'X' symbol stands for …
a) pirate treasure buried here.
b) love and kisses from all in the jungle.
c) require medical assistance.

3 What does the following message mean?

a) urgently need new, fashionable jungle kit, ours no longer trendy.
b) need food and water.
c) grand jumble sale here, this Thursday.

How to ...
set up camp

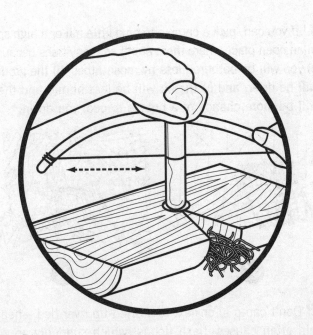

CHOOSING YOUR CAMP SITE

One of the most important things you're going to have to think about on your jungle adventure is establishing a camp. This could be a temporary overnight camp or a more permanent base camp from which you make daily outward explorations into the surrounding jungle terrain. Whichever sort it is, your jungle camp is going to be your home, your shelter and your only refuge from all the things that could make life very unpleasant for you. So it's absolutely vital you get it right.

1 If you can, pick a camp site on a little hill or a high spot in an open place where there aren't so many trees because: **a)** you will be bothered less by mosquitoes; **b)** the ground will be drier; and **c)** the air will be less humid and there will be more chance of a breeze to cool you down.

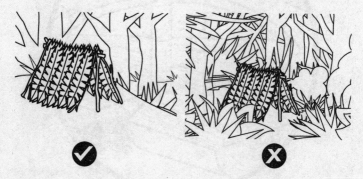

2 Don't camp in or next to a dried-up river bed – heavy rain often causes 'flash floods' which suddenly appear in the form of a huge wall of water rushing along and sweeping away everything in front of it ... including you and your camp site!

3 Avoid camping on well-trodden animal trails. You might end up setting up your shelter on the path the local elephants use on their daily trips to the water hole!

Jungle tale

A scientist working in the African Congo unknowingly built his camp on a hippo run. That night he was awoken by the beasts charging through the undergrowth towards his tent. He leapt out of bed just in time and spent the rest of the night perched in a tree.

Action-Seeker Tip

If you see termites around there's a good chance there'll be trees with dead branches nearby, so take care.

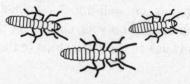

Establishing a camp-site routine

If you're exploring an area of jungle that's really close to the equator you'll find that dawn and dusk occur at the same time each day. You'll also discover that at nightfall there's no gradual getting dark like there is further north. One moment it's light, and a few moments later it's dark. Whumph! Just like that! Not even time to get your jim-jams on. So make sure:

a) you get your camp organized and your shelter constructed (if you've just arrived);

b) you get your fire lit; and

c) you go to the loo

... all before it gets dark!

Jungle weather also tends to follow a pattern each day, with rainstorms regularly taking place each evening just as it's getting dark. What you have to do is adapt your day to these natural conditions, so here's a suggested routine:

Jungle routine

Daybreak: Get up and get busy. Get washed. Go to the loo. Get your fire and brekky organized. Sort out your kit. Tidy up. Begin your trek or your exploration of the area you're camped in.

Morning until midday: Be active. Either trekking or doing jobs in your camp.

Midday: Have a break and chill out. The weather will be at its hottest now. Air your clothes and sleeping bag in the sun (but keep them off the ground!).

Early afternoon: Time to be active again. Wash your clothes or yourself. Collect firewood. Repair equipment. Or simply go trekking.

Mid-afternoon (about 3 pm): If you have been travelling to a new area it's now time to start looking for a suitable camp site. Whatever you do, don't leave it too late! You could end up being caught out by the sudden darkness and having to spend the night in a dangerous and uncomfortable spot.

Evening: Get ready for bed good and early. You need more sleep than usual when you're in the jungle because: **a)** the effort of moving in the intense steamy heat exhausts you very quickly; and **b)** you have to keep up your body's energy and strength to resist the diseases that are more likely to attack you in your new environment.

BUILDING YOUR SHELTER

Once you've chosen your camp site, it's essential that you create some sort of shelter. It will protect you from the rain, biting insects, jungle animals and all the stuff that falls from the forest canopy – fruit, leaves, monkey poo ... that sort of thing.

And during the day the blazing tropical sun will beat down and you'll be desperate for shade.

Action-Seeker Tip

Don't build your shelter under large trees or trees with dead limbs. They may fall and wreck your camp or cause injury, especially if there's a storm. Falling branches kill more jungle visitors than anything else!

You have several shelter-making options. If you're in jungle where bamboo grows, you're lucky! Bamboo is brilliant stuff and you can make hundreds of different things from it, not to mention eating bamboo shoots and drinking bamboo beer while you're at it.

WARNING

Take care when you're handling bamboo because it can split suddenly and sharp splinters can do awful things like going down the back of your fingernails. The edges of leaves can also be razor sharp, causing cuts which will fester in the jungle humidity. And as you cut the bamboo it may bend, then suddenly spring back and smack you in the Orinoco Delta region (ouch!).

Making a bamboo shelter

1 Stick two thick bamboo poles vertically in the ground. The distance between them should be approximately equal to your own height plus the length of an arm.

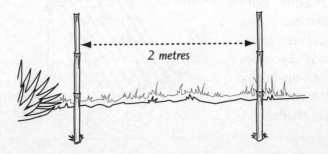

2 metres

2 Find two forked poles (any sort of wood will do) which are about a third of a metre shorter in length than the bamboo. Stick them in the ground about a metre away from the first two poles.

3 Use a length of parachute cord to lash a horizontal 'ridge' pole between each set of posts.

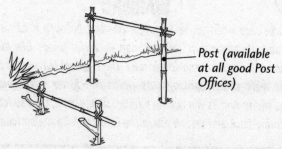

Post (available at all good Post Offices)

4 Use your knife to split a bamboo stem along its length so you end up with two semi-circular halves. Wedge it in the forks of the shorter poles. This will be your rainwater gutter. Block one end with leaves and put something beneath the other to catch the water.

5 Split more bamboo stems and lay them side by side, face-up along the length of the shelter.

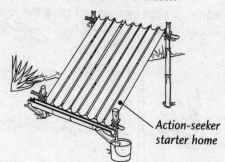

Action-seeker starter home

6 Now lay more split bamboo stems face-down so the two layers interlock. This clever arrangement will give you a superb waterproof roof (or an untidy heap of split bamboo canes).

7 Erect a little 'Bamboo Heaven' sign outside your shelter. (Optional.)

Building a shelter with a leaf roof

If you haven't got lots of bamboo handy you could always try this method:

1 Hammer four solid posts into the ground.

2 Cut notches into the outside of the posts about two thirds of a metre above the ground.

3 Securely lash four horizontal branches to the notches – this will be your bedframe. Finish it off just as you would for your bed (see page 68).

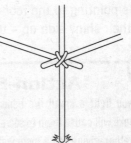

4 Make your roof by lashing together seven more poles.

5 Lash the roof to the upright poles.

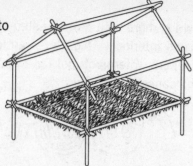

6 Lash more branches horizontally along your roof 'gables'.

7 Gather lots of large leaves (e.g. vine leaves) and make a notch in their stems.

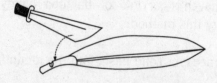

8 Hang them on to the frame by hooking the notch on to the horizontal gable branches. Set the leaves with their stems pointing to the roof ridge, their tips pointing down and their shiny side up – this will help keep off the rain.

Action-Seeker Tip

If you light a small fire beneath the vine leaves, the heat and smoke will cause them to secrete natural oils which will fuse them together, giving you a more waterproof roof (or a huge bonfire).

Making a grass rope

Making both of these shelters requires rope (or cordage as action-seekers call it) for lashing together frames and securing roofs. However, on occasion you may not have this vital resource to hand. You've arrived at your first camp site and, in preparation for building your shelter and stringing up your mozzie net, you begin searching your rucksack for your supply of parachute cord. As you get to the bottom of the bag, still not having found the precious stuff, you suddenly get an image of it sitting on your bedroom floor and, horrified, realize you've left it behind!

Don't panic, action-seeker, you can make your own rope. (It's definitely knot a problem.) It sounds quite complicated but it should only take you a few minutes to get the hang of it. Here's what to do:

1 Collect some handfuls of fresh springy grass, the longer the better.

2 Hold about 12 strands of grass in each hand, between your thumb and fingers.

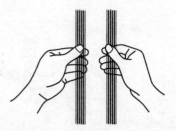

3 Hold the grass in your right hand behind the grass in your left hand so that you make a cross shape.

4 Hold the centre of the cross in your left hand between your thumb and fingers.

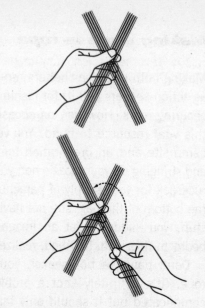

5 With your right hand, grasp the bottom right hand grass and pass it over and through the centre of the cross, then grasp it with your left hand.

6 Still holding the grass tight with your left hand, place your right hand over your left wrist and slide it up until you can grasp the right-hand rope section. Now twist the grass until you've got a strong length of rope.

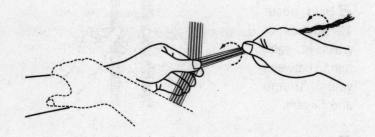

7 Repeat stage 6 with the remaining section of grass.

Now that you've got your rope you need to know how to use it. In other words, how to tie the different sorts of knots and lashes you'll need to use in making things like shelters, slings, traps, belts, boot laces, climbing aids, bridges and fishing nets. Here are a few useful ones to know:

● Reef knot: if there's only one knot you learn, this knot is the one to go for.

● Slippery hitch: for hanging things from branches.

● Overhand knot: another general purpose knot.

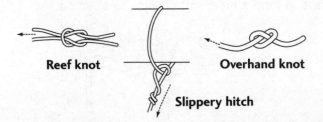

Reef knot   **Overhand knot**

Slippery hitch

BUILDING A BED

It's vital that you sleep off the ground because the jungle is always damp and teeming with insects, reptiles and rodents. The best thing to use is a hammock, but if you haven't got one you can make your own bed. Here's what to do:

1 Cut four poles and drive them firmly into the ground inside your shelter so they make a rectangle. They should be far enough apart and strong enough to support you.

2 Using your knife, cut two poles that are long enough to span the width of the rectangle. They must also be strong enough to support your weight.

3 Lash these poles to the rectangle.

4 Cut lots more poles. Lay them across the two side poles, and lash them securely.

5 Cover the top of your bed frame with broad leaves or grass to form a nice, soft cushion to sleep on.

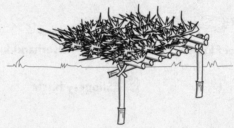

6 Go to bed. Night night! Mind the bugs don't bi— Ooer!

Action-Seeker Tip

All sorts of creepy-crawlies can sneak up on you and your gear while you're sleeping so you must take precautions. On waking and before dressing, check your boots, shoes, pockets and rucksack. Shake out your boots and clothes thoroughly before you put them on.

Jungle tale

In 1946, at the end of WWII, a Japanese soldier called Shoichi Yokoi decided he'd sooner die than be captured alive by American soldiers so he hid out in the jungle on the Pacific island of Guam. In 1972, some Guam locals who were out hunting heard a noise in the reeds next to a river and the next moment a wild-looking man appeared carrying a shrimp trap. It was Yokoi. He'd managed to survive in the jungle for 26 years!

After making himself a trowel out of a cannon shell, Yokoi had dug an underground home in a bamboo grove. His hidey hole, which was reached by a three-metre bamboo ladder, had a kitchen, bamboo-leaf carpets, a loo which emptied into the river, and coconut-shell oil lanterns. Water was easy to get but Yokoi said he always boiled it before drinking it just in case.

He'd lived on mangoes, nuts, crabs, prawns, snails, rats, eels, pigeons, and wild pig and built traps which he baited with grated coconut. He'd even made a rat trap from wire. Yokoi said he liked rat meat and was especially partial to rat liver. Yokoi, who'd been a tailor before the war, had made his own clothes by beating tree bark into flat pieces then stitching it into suits and shirts. He made the buttons from the disused case of his plastic torch. To make his fires Yokoi used a lens, but lost this, so he then made a wooden hand-drill fire starter. Doctors who examined Yokoi after he was found said he was as fit as a fiddle!

MAKING FIRE

Even if it's hot, building a fire always makes you feel lots better when you're out in the wilderness, whether it's jungle, snow-covered mountain or desert. In the jungle, your fire will keep you warm on cool nights, keep insects and dangerous wild animals away, cook your food, dry out your damp clothing, and provide you with light. So don't be without one!

Action-Seeker Tip

If there are any termite mounds nearby, break off some chunks and drop them in your fire. The smoke it creates is extra- effective as a mosquito deterrent.

The trick to making a good fire is to start with teensy-weensy bits of fuel, then move on to bigger and bigger fuel, until you end up putting on thick logs.

What you need:

a) Tinder. The stuff you light first. It catches fire quickly and should blaze up as soon as it's touched by a flame. For tinder use dry moss, tree bark, dry grass and dry leaves. Prepare your tinder by using your machete or knife to carefully trim it into small pieces (with lots of tinder loving care).

b) Kindling. The small fuel you add to your fire as soon as the tinder is flaming; mainly dry sticks and leaves.

c) Main fuel. The larger sticks that are thicker than a finger (but will soon be brighter than a professor).

d) Large fuel. The big logs that you use to keep your fire going all night.

e) Some matches, a lighter or a fire drill and bow (see page 74).

WARNING

When you're gathering fuel, watch out for snakes and any other nasties you might disturb.

Make sure you have a good supply of tinder, kindling and main fuel close at hand before you begin making your fire. You don't want to have to go wandering off to look for more fuel halfway through the job. When you are ready to make your fire, here's what to do:

1 Site your fire carefully. If it's too exposed to breezes, the heat will be blown away. And don't build it too close to your shelter or it may go up in flames. (The shelter, not your fire ... *that is* supposed to go up in flames.)

2 Clear a circle on the ground (about a metre across) to cut down the chances of your fire spreading and getting out of control.

3 Make a fire wall with logs or rocks. This will help to direct the heat where you want it to go (i.e. towards you and your chilly little tootsies). It will also cut down the amount of sparks flying around.

4 Make a fire platform by laying some dry wood on the ground. This will keep your tinder and kindling off the damp ground.

5 Put a couple of handfuls of small kindling on the platform to make a little teepee shape with a gap inside. This teepee kindling should be about the same thickness as the average matchstick.

Rock wall for heat reflection and windbreaking (but not breaking wind)

Action-Seeker Tip

The more heat you create when you start your fire, the more successful it's going to be.

6 Put some tinder 'inside' the teepee and set light to it. The flames should soon reach the kindling. When it's blazing, add more kindling.

7 Once the fire is blazing really well, carefully lay on some small sticks. Once these sticks are burning, your fire should stay well and truly lit.

8 Strip to your underwear, paint your face with mud and dance around your fire, slapping your bottom and making ridiculous whooping noises. (Optional.)

Making fire without matches

You decide to try your hand at fishing, so you go down to the river and in no time at all you hook a real whopper. It struggles like crazy and as you attempt to haul it out of the water you suddenly lose your footing in the slippery mud of the riverbank and plunge into its murky waters (aaaargh ... sploosh!). You're relieved to discover it's not too deep so, being a determined, never-say-die sort of action-seeker, you continue to battle the giant fish despite the fact that it's pulling you this way and that! Finally, completely exhausted, you haul it ashore, eagerly looking forward to cooking it and eating it, especially as you're now hungrier than ever! You begin looking for your matches so that you can get the fire going but, as you do, you realize they've been in your pocket the entire time you were catching the fish and are now completely soaked and useless! And even worse, you now discover that your trusty lighter fell out of your pocket some time during the struggle and is now lost for all time somewhere on the river bed. What are you to do? You can't possibly eat the fish raw and you must have a fire to dry yourself out and keep you company during the night. Don't despair, action-seeker! Do it like the primitive folk do and make your fire with an ingenious fire bow.

This device is like a bow and arrow, with the bow string twisted once around the arrow (the drill) so that a backward and forward motion of the bow produces a fast-turning arrow. The sharp end of the arrow is pressed down into a dent cut in a log where the frantic rubbing creates lots of heat (and a sore wrist). Just the thing to give yourself some cheery flames to fry your fish and warm your damp cockles during those long lonely nights in the jungle.

What you need:

a) A bendy bow stick about as thick as your little finger, half a metre long.

b) A length of string to tie to your bow stick so it's good and taut.

c) A dry spinning stick with rounded ends, about 25 cm long.

d) A dry log for your spinning stick to spin on.

e) A hand support to stabilize your spinning stick as you rotate it – a stone with a groove or a piece of wood with a hole in will do.

f) A good supply of dry tinder.

g) Plenty of fuel for your main fire.

h) A collection of merry songs to sing around your campfire once you've got it blazing. (Optional.)

What to do:

1 Use your knife or a sharp stone to dig a little dent in your log. This is to spin the tip of your stick in.

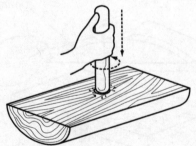

2 Next to the dent, cut a V-shaped notch. This is for your hot ash to fall through and onto the waiting tinder.

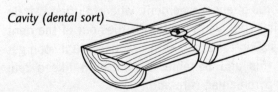

Cavity (dental sort)

3 Put some dry tinder next to the V-shaped notch.

4 Place your foot on the base log to keep it firm.

5 Twist the drill tightly in the bow string.

6 Place its lower end in the dent and hold it there with the hand support.

7 Start to drill slowly using a smooth and regular backwards and forwards action but gradually speed up the pace and put on more pressure.

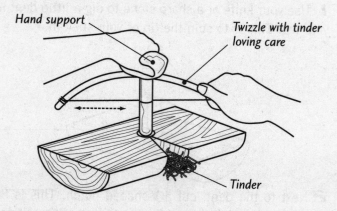

Hand support

Twizzle with tinder loving care

Tinder

Some words of encouragement: when you first twizzle your spinning stick you may find it flies out of the dent a few times. Don't despair, with practice you'll soon get a feel for this and be able to control it like a real prehistoric pyromaniac (fire-addict).

8 After a few minutes (or months) the friction and heat caused by twizzling your notch should begin to make the base log smoke like mad.

9 When it does, do about 20 more twizzles, then carefully lift your bow away.

10 You should now see some brown embers glowing in the dent. Gently tip them on to the kindling and begin blowing on it until flames appear.

Your smart new blazer

11 Gradually begin adding fuel to your fire until you've got a really good blaze going (then call the fire brigade).

WARNING

Action-seeker, you may be tempted to practise fire-making before you go on your adventure. If you do, get a responsible adult (available in most good sitting rooms) to help you. Fire-making can be a very dangerous task!

HAVE YOU BEEN PAYING ATTENTION?

1 The best place to set up your camp is ...
a) a dried-up river bed.
b) the fast lane of the trans-Brazilian highway.
c) a small hill where the air is fresher.

2 When you build your fire, set up your kindling in the shape of ...
a) a teepee.
b) a Japanese pagoda.
c) a telly tubby.

3 For kindling the best things to use are ...
a) twigs.
b) Twiglets.
c) fire ants.

How to ...
get water
and food

You'll have fewer problems finding food and water in the jungle than you would if you were trekking in the desert, moorlands or mountains. Nevertheless, as there's no telling what sort of desperate, life-threatening survival situations you might find yourself in during your expedition, it's absolutely crucial that you know how to get food and water from the wild. Luckily the jungle is bursting with scrummy things to eat and drink – if you know where to look.

FINDING WATER

You're staggering through the jungle, the weather's boiling hot and you've got a thirst you could photograph. Your tongue feels like a slice of stale bread which has been stuck to the roof of your mouth with super glue. You're dizzy, your vision's blurred, you can't remember the last time you needed a tiddle and you can't think straight. What you're suffering from, action-seeker, is known as dehydration. Bit by bit, your entire body is drying up! 'But this is the jungle!' you croak. 'Or *rain*forest, as it's also called. And it's wet, wet, wet. So why do I feel like a jellyfish in a microwave?'

The dry facts
a) Your body loses fluid as a result of heat, stress, and exertion, especially when you're in really hot places like the jungle ... and you must replace this fluid.

b) Even in cold, damp places you need to drink at least two litres of water a day to function effectively.

c) You can survive for three weeks without food but only three days without water.

21 days   **3 days**

So one of your main tasks is to keep yourself well supplied with water.

WARNING

If you see local jungle folk crouching down and drinking directly from streams and rivers ... don't copy them! Over hundreds of years and many generations, their internal immune systems have built up defences against all the bugs. Yours, action-seeker, hasn't!

Getting water from plants

Here are a few plants that can supply you with water in the jungle:

Green bamboo Bend a green-bamboo stalk, tie it to another stalk, and cut off the top. The water will drip out of it throughout the night, so put something there to catch it (or just lie underneath it with your mouth open!). Water from green bamboo is clear and doesn't smell.

WARNING

Don't store water you've got from plants for more than 24 hours because it will begin to ferment (turn to alcohol).

Banana trees Cut the banana tree with your machete so that you leave a short stump sticking out of the ground. Hollow the inside of the stump to make a bowl shape. After a few hours, the banana tree's roots will fill the bowl with water. The first bowls of water will be slightly bitter-tasting but it's still safe to drink. After you've emptied the bowl, put a banana leaf over it to stop the water evaporating (and to stop creepy-crawlies from holding swimming galas in it). The banana stump will continue to give you water for three days (before it finally realizes the cruel trick you've played on it).

Water vines These are about 10 cm thick. If you cut a metre-long piece it will produce a stream of clear, fruity or watery-tasting running water.

WARNING

If you've picked the wrong vine, the water will be sappy and only drip out. It will also be bitter and cloudy. Do not drink this sap – it can be highly poisonous!

Pulpy plants You can get water from plants with moist pulpy centres such as the papaya (or paw paw). Cut off a section of the plant and squeeze or mash up the pulp so that the moisture runs out. Catch the liquid in a container.

Plant roots Plants like the African umbrella tree (which you can also pick really nice umbrellas from) may provide water. Dig the roots out of the ground, cut them into short pieces, and smash the pulp so that the moisture runs out.

Rainwater The leaves of many plants make bowl shapes which rainwater collects in. You can also find water in the crevices made by tree trunks and their branches.

Following animals to water

Becoming a wildlife watcher may also lead you to desperately needed water. Watch out for these tell-tale signs...

• Birds drink at dawn and dusk. When they fly straight and low, they're heading for water. When they fly from tree to tree, resting frequently, they're returning from drinking (and when they lay on their backs with their legs in the air, they're completely sozzled).

• Animals following well-used trails may indicate that there is a water supply nearby. (For instance, troops of howler monkeys carrying bottles of sparkling spring water are a sure sign that there's a good mini-market within walking distance.)

Action-Seeker Tip

If you come to a pool in the jungle that has animal skeletons close to it, it's probably not a good idea to drink the water.

- Bees or ants going into a hole in a tree may be a sign that there's water in it. Scoop out the water, suck it up through a hollow tube or stuff a cloth in the hole then wring it from the cloth.·
- Human tracks are likely to lead to a well, water hole (or wine bar).

Purifying water

Water you get from rivers and streams may contain general muck and bits of rock (which makes it cloudy), parasitic worms (which set up home in your insides and make you ill) and bacteria and viruses (which can give you diseases like polio) so you must definitely purify it by boiling it for at least three minutes or using water sterilizing tablets. You can also strain water by filtering it through bamboo tubes filled with leaves. You could try tying your trouser cuffs, filling your trousers with sand, hanging them from a tree and then pouring the water through them and catching it in a container. (But remember to take your trousers off before you do this.)

HAVE YOU BEEN PAYING ATTENTION?

1 Once you've cut a water vine it will produce ...
a) a blockbusting action movie.
b) a stream of water.
c) a stream of abuse.

2 If you see bees or ants going into a hole in a tree it may indicate that ...
a) it contains water.
b) there's a really good party going on in there.
c) they're shy.

3 Water that you collect from streams and rivers often contains ...
a) scuba divers.
b) parasites.
c) yellow plastic ducks.

FINDING FOOD

It's day ten of your expedition and so far, give or take a few little upsets (see pages 23, 29, 36, 42, 45, 73), things have gone pretty well. But then you get out of bed and are shattered to find that, during the night, a couple of hungry orang-utans have stolen your entire supply of food. It was meant to last you another ten days! And you're hundreds of kilometres from the nearest shop! Already feeling peckish, you spend the morning looking for any scraps of food the orang-utans may have left behind but you don't find a thing. By lunchtime you're beginning to feel very hungry, by teatime you're absolutely starving and, by the next morning, your stomach feels as though it's trying to eat itself! There's nothing for it, you'll have to live off the jungle. It's teeming with all sorts of animals, and plants are everywhere. All you have to do is catch them or harvest them and you'll be fine.

You can eat almost anything that crawls, swims, walks, or flies (apart from jumbo jets and school librarians) so all you have to do is choose your prey, stalk it, trap it, clobber it, cook it and eat it. It's a piece of ~~cake~~ steak. However, action-seeker, you're in the jungle. And in the jungle meaty things go bad very quickly. So it's better to forget about things like eating deer, elephants and monkeys and concentrate on some things that are easier to catch (and which won't fight back).

Finding and trapping insects

There are hundreds of thousands of insects in the jungle and many of them taste good and are full of life-giving nourishment. Eating an insect can often give you three times as much protein as eating a couple of kilos of steak (but only if the insect happens to be the size of a Great Dane puppy).

You can find insects – including ants, termites, beetles and grubs (beetle larvae) – living inside and underneath rotting logs. Try investigating insect nests on or underneath the ground. Grassy areas, such as jungle clearings, are also good areas to search because the insects are easy to spot. Once you've caught your insects remove their legs, antennae, wings and stings before you eat them.

A selection of insects you can eat

Ants and ant larvae Very tasty. Boil them first to get rid of their formic acid 'sting'.

Action-Seeker Tip

If you're out of lemon juice, larger ants can be squeezed so that their acid drips onto your fresh wild salad. People in Thailand use them this way.

Caterpillars Fine, but avoid the hippies (i.e. the hairy and psychedelic kinds).

Crickets, stick insects and grasshoppers Give you protein, calories and fat.

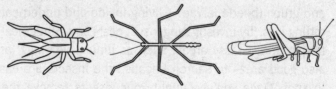

Earthworms Have lots of protein and can be eaten raw.

Action-Seeker Tip

Keep the earthworms for a couple of days and feed them on fresh vegetation before you eat them. (Though, you may become so fond of them that you can't bear to gobble them up.)

Honey bees Regarded as a tasty snack in many parts of the world. Boil them first though to destroy their sting.

Moths The ones which fly around your lights and fire are OK to eat. They taste a bit like almonds.

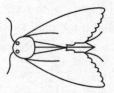

Termites The second most popular insect dish in the world after grasshoppers and they're easy to catch.

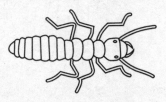

Catching termites chimpanzee style

Jungle pygmies from the African Congo region use the following method to catch termites. They first picked up the idea when they saw chimpanzees doing it. (The chimps first read about it in a jungle survival manual.)

First, find a termite mound.

Then block up all the entrance and exit holes but one and poke a stick into the open hole.

WARNING

Snakes and scorpions sometimes squat in termite nests so take care when you're poking.

The angry termites will come rushing out of the hole (carrying frying pans and dressed in their pyjamas). Many of them will cling to the stick. (A ready-made termite kebab ... what more could you want?) Scoop the rest into a container and keep them until needed.

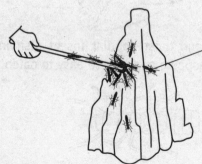

Termites, aka white ants (yes, that's right, antagonize them)

Action-Seeker Tip

Another way to get the termites is to pick up their mound and lower it into water. In no time they'll come charging out ready to be scooped up and roasted.

Creepy-crawlies to avoid eating

Hairy insects
Brightly coloured insects The bright colours are often nature's way of saying, 'Gerroff! I taste like poo and you'll die if you eat me!'
Caterpillars and insects that have a really strong smell Another public health warning.
Spiders
Ticks, flies, and mosquitoes In fact, any insects that carry diseases (or concealed handguns).

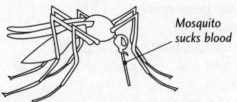

Mosquito sucks blood

Cooking insects

Some people eat their insects raw. However, if you prefer yours cooked, here are a couple of scrummy recipes to try:

Crunchy roast bugs

This way of cooking insects keeps all the beneficial nutrients in their shells, wastes nothing and prevents them from shrivelling up.

What to do:

1 Heat some sand on your fire.

2 Put the sand and the insects in a container.

3 Shake the sand so it covers the insects.

4 Keep shaking until they go deep brown and begin to look brittle, then take them out and eat them.

Action-Seeker Tip

If you can't find any sand, this recipe works just as well with dry earth.

Fried grasshoppers

What to do:

1 Remove head, wings and legs.

2 Melt a knob of butter in a frying pan over a medium flame.

3 Add grasshoppers.

4 Fry gently for 3–4 minutes.

5 Remove from pan and season to taste.

HAVE YOU BEEN PAYING ATTENTION?

1 Many insects are of full of ...

a) sage-and-onion stuffing.

b) protein.

c) their own self-importance.

2 The best place to find insects is ...

a) in the hair of TV celebs.

b) under rotting logs.

c) in traffic wardens' armpits.

3 The best way to catch termites is ...

a) by rounding them up with border collies.

b) blocking up all the holes in their nests bar one.

c) picking them off with bows and arrows.

CATCHING FISH

Fish are plentiful in streams and rivers and they're full of the proteins and fats that will keep you alive. They're easy to catch if you know a few things about them. For example:

- They feed heavily before a storm.
- They aren't likely to feed after a storm when the water is muddy.
- They're attracted to light at night.
- When there is a heavy current, fish go to less fast-flowing parts of the river.
- Fish gather where there are deep pools, under overhanging branches and around underwater plants, logs or other objects that give them shelter.

WARNING

You must cook all freshwater fish to kill the parasites that live in them.

Rod, line and hook fishing

Tie a line to a stick and attach a hook to the end of the line. Bait the hook with a worm, insect or slug, then dangle it in the water. When the fish takes the bait, haul it out of the water. Lots of time and patience is required with this method of fishing so you may prefer to use an alternative method.

Spear fishing

Cut a long, straight stick. Sharpen the end to a point, or lash your knife to it. Stand in waist-deep water where the fish are large and gather in groups. Place your spear point into the water and slowly move it towards a fish of your choice. Then, with a sudden thrust, pin your fish to the stream bed. Don't try and lift the fish with your spear, because it will probably slip off and you will lose it. Simply hold the spear with one hand and grab hold of the fish with the other.

Action-Seeker Tip

Don't throw your spear, especially if your knife is tied to the tip. If you lose your knife you may end up in big trouble!

Fish basket trap

Push several sticks into a hole scooped out in the ground. Place a stone in the middle of them and fan them out. Now tie the sticks together with vines to make a funnel shape. Close the top, leaving a hole at the other end large enough for the fish to swim into. Your fish trap is now ready. Take it to the river and place it in the water quite near to the bank. Anchor it with a stone.

Stakeout

Push a couple of sticks into the bottom of a pond or stream with their tops just below the surface. Tie string between them, slightly below the surface. Tie two shorter cords and tie baited hooks to this string. Go off and do something useful, then return to your stakeout a bit later to see if any fish have taken the bait.

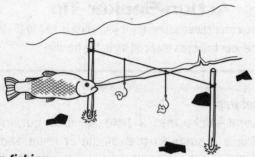

Chop fishing

You do this at night. Stand in the water and shine your torch on the surface. The curious fish will come to investigate. When they do, clobber them with the blunt edge of your machete (you heartless monster).

Preparing and cooking your fish

If your fish isn't already dead, kill it by walloping it on the back of its head with a stick or stone, then get it ready to eat as soon as you can. Fish go off (meaning that they decay, not that they explode!) very quickly after they've died, especially in the heat of the jungle and eating sick or rotten fish can make you very ill.

The danger signs to watch out for are: sunken eyes and strange smell (in the fish, not you); dodgy colour (the gills of the fish should be red or pink and the scales should be bright and shiny); and a slimy body (yuk), rather than a moist or wet one.

Action-Seeker Tip

Press your thumb into the flesh to make a dent. If the dent stays there after you've taken your thumb away, the fish is rotten. (And if it yells abuse at you, you'll need to hit it with the stick again.)

If your fish shows any of these signs there's obviously something really *fishy* about it, so don't eat it. However, if it's OK, it's now time to prepare it. Here's how:

Scrape the scales off your fish, moving the blunt end of your knife from tail to head.

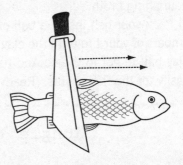

Then take your fish and slit its belly from the anal fin to the head.

Carefully pull out its internal organs and cut off the head and tail and bury them. (Think about saving the eyes though, they'll see you through the week.) Separate the ribs from the flesh using the point of your knife.

Now it's ready for cooking. There are lots of methods to choose from:

a) Pierce your fish through with a stick and then cook it over your open fire.

b) Boil your fish with its skin on. This will get the most goodness out of it. The fats and oil are under its skin and, by boiling it, you can save its juices for a tasty and nourishing broth.

c) Pack your fish inside a ball of clay, then bury it in the embers of your fire until the clay hardens. Break open the clay ball to get to the cooked fish. If the meat flakes off easily (or the fish shouts, 'Ready!'), you'll know it's done.

Jungle tale

When the rivers are at their lowest, the South American Huaroni Indians build dams of plaited reeds across them. Then they get leaves from the barbasco plant which they crush and drop in the river upstream from the dam. The leaves release a chemical which removes the oxygen from the water, causing fish to suffocate. The fish float to the surface and drift downriver to be caught in the dam. The Huaroni put the fish on raised wooden racks and roast them over charcoal fires. They call the rack a barbasco, after the plant they killed the fish with. When the Spanish invaders travelled to the jungles of South America, they borrowed the name for this cooking device, but changed it slightly ... to barbecue! Which is where we get the name we use today.

GETTING FOOD FROM JUNGLE PLANTS

Lots of fruit and vegetables that you can buy in supermarkets, like coconuts, bananas and mangoes, were originally found in the jungle. And there are more where they came from: some grow underground in the form of roots, some as edible leaves, and others as nuts and fruits on the bushes and trees. So if you're looking for food, you needn't starve. What's more, quite a lot of jungle plants, such as coconuts (see page 103) serve loads of other useful purposes too. Eco-aware jungle dwellers have known this for thousands of years, making the most of every part of many plants, and wasting nothing.

WARNING

*Before you start grazing on the jungle's green goodies, you must learn which things are safe to eat and which aren't. Generally speaking, avoid plants that: **a)** have milky sap; **b)** have single berries that are bright red, orange or shiny black; and **c)** have an unpleasant smell.*

Plants you can eat

Breadfruit Found on the edge of jungles in the West Indies and Pacific islands.

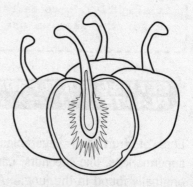

● Grows on tall trees with dark-green leaves.

● A large, round, dark-green fruit, which you can bake on the embers of your campfire. You can also dry and slice it for using later on. (Hence the saying: 'the best thing since sliced breadfruit'.)

Other uses:

a) Use its sap as glue, and to seal leaks.

b) Smear it on twigs to trap small birds. The moment they land on it they become completely stuck (or fly away with the entire tree attached to them).

Yams Found in jungles all over the world.

● Grow on vines with heart- or arrow-shaped leaves that creep along the ground. Boil the roots and eat them as a vegetable. (Hmm, delicious, yam yam.)

Mangoes Found in jungles in India, Burma and Malaysia. They're also grown on farms in most other tropical countries.

● Some are red, others are yellow or orange, and some are a mixture of all these colours. They grow on high trees with dark-green leaves. Eat the flesh raw or roast the seed kernel and eat it.

Papaya or pawpaw Found in open, sunny places in jungles all around the world.

● Grow directly from the trunk of small trees.

● Look like small green pumpkins and turn yellow when ripe.

● Remove the seeds, eat it raw, roast it or boil it. Contains lots of vitamin C.

Other uses:

a) Rub the milky juice on tough meat (e.g. crocodile) to make it more tender.

b) Put on cuts and scratches to help them heal.

WARNING

Don't get the milky sap from the unripe fruit in your eyes. It's really painful and can cause blindness.

Bananas (and plantains) Found at the edges of jungles everywhere.

● Big plants with massive leaves at the top and large clusters of hanging flowers.

● Eat the fruits raw, fried, boiled or baked. (Take the yellow wrappers off first though.) Boil their flowers and eat them like a vegetable. (The centre or 'heart' of the plant is edible all year round, cooked or raw.)

Other uses:

a) Use the layers of the lower third of the plants to cover coals to roast food.

b) Use their stumps to collect water in.

c) Use their leaves to wrap other food for cooking or storage.

WARNING

Don't leave the yellow wrappers lying around or cartoon characters may slip on them.

Bamboos Found in jungles almost everywhere.

● Woody grasses that grow up to 15 metres tall.

● The young shoots of almost all bamboos can be eaten raw or cooked.

● Raw shoots have a slightly bitter taste that is removed by boiling.

● Boil the seeds like rice, or bash them to mix with water and make into cakes.

Other uses:

a) Build shelters (see page 61) or make containers, ladles, spoons and various other cooking utensils.

b) Make tools and weapons. You can also make a strong bow by splitting the bamboo and joining several pieces together.

WARNING

If you put green bamboo on your campfire it may explode (BAM BAM BAM BAM Boo ... just like that).

COCONUT MAGIC

You've been trekking for days. You're desperately thirsty and hungry and your food and water has all gone. You're scratched and battered and have got a couple of deep cuts that might go septic if they're left exposed much longer. You've lost all your equipment but the clothes you're wearing, a blanket, your machete and your matches. You've nothing to sleep in, no tent, no sleeping bag, no mosquito net. It looks like there's going to be a storm later in the day and, when it comes, you're going to have nothing between you and the torrential rain and wind. You also know that the moment the storm finishes, the mosquitoes will begin biting! You won't be able to go on much longer and now feel like falling in a heap on the ground and giving up. But then you suddenly come across dozens of trees with narrow, tall trunks and clusters of really enormous leaves at the top. Many of the leaves are at least six metres long. The trees are coconut palms. And, if you know how to make the most of them, they'll save your life.

Food and drink

Great news! The liquid inside young coconuts contains the precious water you desperately need to replace those vital body fluids you've sweated out as you've struggled through the jungle. It's also rich in sugar and vitamins. The delicious white flesh is packed with energy-giving nutrients.

Not so great news! Before you can get to these goodies there are a couple of problems to be dealt with first...

Problem one

The coconuts scattered on the ground are old ones. Their flesh is hard and difficult to eat. But worse, there's hardly any water in them, and the liquid that is in them will make you desperate for the loo (obviously something of a problem when the nearest public convenience is at least three weeks' walk away). The coconuts that you need are the young ones. And they're at the top of the trees (wouldn't you just know it!). To get them, you must climb.

Don't worry, it's easy when you know how. Here's what to do:

Climbing a coconut tree

Before you start, take off your boots and socks. You have to climb barefoot. Wear a shirt though, to protect your skin from the tree's rough bark.

If the tree trunk is wide and leans slightly
Put your hands close to each other on the back of the trunk and put one foot above the other on the trunk.

Then press on the front of the trunk with your toes and the balls of your feet while pulling on the back of the trunk with your hands. Start to 'walk' up the trunk, first moving your feet and then your hands.

If the tree trunk is narrow and vertical

'Flex' your legs on each side of the tree with the soles of your feet 'wrapped' around the trunk and pressing hard. You'll look a bit like a frog. Then place one hand on the back of the trunk and the other hand on the front, level with your chest.

Press hard with both of them and pull your legs up whilst 'squeezing' the trunk with your hands and feet. Move your hands up and keep repeating the sequence.

When you get to the top there are three ways to get the coconuts:

a) Hold yourself with one hand on the back of the trunk whilst squeezing it with your flexed legs. Use your free hand to grab a coconut. Twist it until the stem breaks.

b) Grab a hold of one of the palm leaves, hold on to it with your legs flexed and gripping the trunk, and use your free hand to twist a coconut.

c) Stand up on top of the leaves. From there you can easily grab all the coconuts without effort.

WARNING

Don't carry your machete with you as you climb a coconut tree. It could be really dangerous. If you do feel that you need it, attach a rope to it then pull it up when you get to the top.

Going down

Keep your legs and feet in the flexed position and move your hands one after the other behind the trunk, letting the soles of your feet drag against the tree as you descend.

Action-Seeker Tip

Don't try carrying all of your coconut harvest with you as you climb down, it could make holding the trunk a bit tricky. Just throw them down, but be careful if you've got companions down there!

OK, you've got your nuts. Now to solve...

Problem two

All the coconut goodies are encased in a very hard shell that many people find difficult to crack open without spilling that lifesaving milk. So here's what you must do next:

Using your machete to open a coconut

Hold the coconut in one hand so that its middle section rests in the palm of your hand with the tip at one end and the eyes at the other, then give the side of the coconut shell a few sharp taps with the blunt edge of your knife. The coconut should crack open cleanly and separate into two halves.

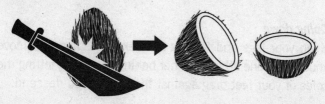

Action-Seeker Tip

As you open this first coconut you may lose some of the milk. But don't worry, there's plenty more where that came from. And all you have to do is use the empty half of a coconut you've already cracked to catch the next lot of milk in.

Eat the flesh of the coconuts raw. It will give you lots of energy. Quench your thirst by drinking the 'milk' of the coconut.

Action-Seeker Tip

Pick coconuts when they're green and the size of a grapefruit. That's when they're at their best for eating and drinking from.

OK, you've filled your tum but now that storm's on the way. Time to...

Build a shelter and get comfy

1 Use the trunks of smaller (or fallen) coconut trees to make a frame for a shelter (see page 61).

2 Use the palm leaves to make thatching for your roof and walls, and matting for the floors.

3 Use your machete to shred dried coconut fibres. Stuff your blanket with them to make a comfy mattress.

Replenish your supplies and equipment

a) Use the dried coconut shells to make bowls, cups and containers for storing things in.

b) Cut out the central veins of the leaves, then bunch them together to make a broom.

c) Build up a stock of coconut oil for future cooking. To get the coconut oil from the coconut, put the white coconut flesh in the sun, heat it over a slow fire, or boil it in a pot of water.

d) Use the husks' fibres to weave rope.

e) Use the large stumps of fallen coconut trees to store food and supplies in.

f) Make liquid strainers from the fine leaf bases.

As night falls

Make a campfire using the dried husks of the old fallen coconuts you find on the ground. Start the fire with tinder made from the hairy bits of the husks. Keep the fire going all night – mosquitoes hate the smoke.

Make a lamp by burning coconut oil in a coconut shell. Choose the most intelligent-looking coconut in the bunch and spend the evening swapping campfire tales and discussing the meaning of life. (Optional.)

Moving on

You may find that the bit of jungle you're in is quite near the sea. So if no one turns up to rescue you, you might want to build a raft to escape on. Use your coconut husk ropes to lash coconut tree trunks together, then fasten lots of empty coconut husks to the raft as they make brilliant floats. Make a palm-leaf screen to keep off the hot sun, stock up on fresh coconuts, coconut milk and coconut oil ... and off you go.

HAVE YOU BEEN PAYING ATTENTION?

1 Fish tend to ...

a) hang out on street corners.

b) gather in deep pools.

c) be attracted to light at night.

2 The moment you get your fish on land ...
a) give it a good telling off.
b) clobber it with a stick.
c) throw it back in the river.

3 Breadfruit sap is really useful for ...
a) tiling your bathroom.
b) sealing leaks.
c) controlling difficult-to-manage hairdos.

4 When papaya are ripe they turn ...
a) into huge purple butterflies.
b) yellow.
c) the other cheek.

5 In each ripe coconut that you crack open, you'll find ...
a) a joke and a plastic toy.
b) some nutritious and refreshing liquid.
c) the Lost City of Atlantis.

6 You can use the trunks of coconut trees to make ...
a) delicious soup.
b) a frame for a shelter.
c) stylish swimwear i.e. trunks.

How to ...
cope with
jungle nasties

Some people believe the jungle is teeming with horrendous creatures whose one idea of having a good time is to track down any human beings who are stupid enough to wander into the rainforest, then kill them in the most painful way possible.

This isn't true. Thousands of action-seekers regularly visit jungles all over the world and come away completely unharmed after having had a brilliant jungle adventure. Nevertheless, there *are* nasties in the jungle, just as there are nasties in the world's deserts, mountains, oceans and big cities. Some of them pop up in the form of creepy-crawlies and others in the form of big animals such as tigers, crocodiles, snakes and elephants (but fortunately attacks by those creatures are rare). The trick is knowing what the nasties are, avoiding them and dealing with them if necessary.

DEALING WITH CREEPY-CRAWLIES

Beating down mosquitoes

The most dangerous animal you'll meet in the jungle isn't a puma, a tiger or a crocodile. It's a mosquito. If you added up all the people killed in every single war in history you still wouldn't come anywhere near the number that have been killed by mosquitoes. These flying insects spread the deadly disease known as malaria when they bite you and suck your blood.

Some things you should know about mosquitoes

a) There are over 2,700 different types of mosquito in the world. The ones you meet in the jungle are the most dangerous.

b) Mosquitoes are attracted to heat, light, sweat, body smells and the gas we breathe out (carbon dioxide). (So ideally you should hold your breath the entire time you're in the jungle.)

c) People who don't sweat so much don't get as many mosquito bites.

d) A mosquito can't see you if you're more than ten metres away but it can smell you from over 30 metres away.

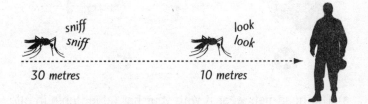

sniff
sniff

look
look

30 metres   10 metres

e) Only female mosquitoes bite, but as they're so titchy it's quite difficult to tell which are which.

f) Some mosquitoes prefer to feed on animals, while others prefer the blood of human beings. Some go for either.

g) You'll know when mosquitoes are about because you'll hear the noise of their buzz coming towards you (unless they've decided to catch a later one).

Preventing mozzie attacks

To guard against the menace of mosquitoes, keep in mind the three 'A's – Awareness, Avoidance and Anti-malaria medicine – then follow this advice:

1 Always use your mosquito net (not for catching mozzies but as a shield against them).

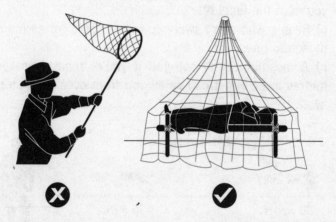

a) The head-net: wear it with your hat (a[veil]able in all good outdoor shops).
b) The bed-net: tuck it in well to stop them getting into bed with you.

2 Use insect repellent on your skin, your clothes, your camping gear and your mosquito nets.

3 Wear protective clothing such as long-sleeved shirts and long trousers to reduce your chances of being bitten.

4 Stay away from swampy areas, where mosquitoes breed.

5 If a mozzy lands on you, don't dither. Squidge it immediately!

Action-Seeker Tip

If a mozzy's hovering around you, wondering which bit of you to bite, clap your hands just below it. The wave of air caused by the clap will cause it to drop down. When it does, show your appreciation by giving it another round of applause ... splat!

Dealing with leeches

You've just hacked your way through a swampy area overgrown with all sorts of low-growing, rain-soaked trees and bushes that have constantly brushed against your body and face. Exhausted, you've now paused to rest in a clearing and are admiring some rather beautiful butterflies that are feeding on a bush. You suddenly feel a strange sensation on your leg, then another on your arm and more on your neck. You roll up your trouser leg and are alarmed to see that a gruesome, slug-like creature has attached itself to your ankle. Then you reach up and discover that another is clinging to your neck. In fact the horrendous things are all over you! With horror, you realize that dozens of leeches are clinging to your flesh and sucking your blood! Yes, you're under attack from the dreaded Count Draculas of the worm world. In panic you reach down and grasp the nearest leech and attempt to pull it off. But to your dismay its jaws are so firmly clamped into your flesh that you're unable to budge it! What should you do now?

Some disgusting things you should know about leeches

a) Leeches are bloodsucking parasites and are close rellies of earthworms.

b) They've got suckers on their head and on their back end. A leech's mouth is inside its front sucker and its back sucker is next to its bottom (just in case you ever wish to give the leech a smack in the chops and aren't sure which end to wallop).

c) When they're looking for victims, they raise their head and the upper part of their body and wave them about and sniff the air until they smell blood. Then they move rapidly towards you, climb up your boots, then either scoot up your leg or just bury themselves in your socks.

d) Once it's found a juicy part of your flesh to suck, the leech holds its sucker in place by making its body go all stiff. Then, using its semicircular jaws and numerous sharp teeth, it bites your skin and squirts out sticky mucus which 'glues' the sucker to your flesh. Once that's sorted the leech injects you with a chemical that stops your blood clotting and it begins drinking. Even if you manage to pull the leech off, you won't stop bleeding for hours.

e) Bacteria from a leech's gut can infect the bite wound, so after you've been tangoed you may get itching and soreness.

f) Leeches can drink several times their own body weight in blood at one go.

g) Some leeches feed on the blood of humans and other mammals, while others attack fish, frogs, turtles and birds (so don't take it personally).

Getting rid of leeches

Take a burning stick, hold the glowing end against the leech, then watch it crumple and sizzle as it falls to the ground all cheesed-off and charred.

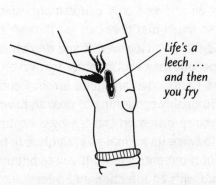

Life's a leech ... and then you fry

WARNING

If you try to remove leeches by just firmly pulling them off there is a chance their head will come off, leaving their jaws in the bite which could then turn poisonous.

Action-Seeker Tip

Before you set off on your trek, smear your legs with bath soap, eucalyptus oil, tropical-strength insect repellent or lemon juice (but not all at the same time or you'll end up smelling like an explosion in a fragrance factory).

Some irritating little creatures to avoid

Sand fleas If you get bitten by a sand flea, you get sand-flea fever. The bite will be very itchy but you must not scratch it as this will only cause more infection. Sand fleas are so small that they can get through the holes in your mosquito net. However, if you drench the net with insect repellent they won't bother trying.

Centipedes Centipedes are quite stroppy and can move very fast (probably something to do with having all those legs). If you're bitten on the leg by a centipede it can swell up to twice its normal size. Centipede bites can be really painful but aren't fatal. If you're bitten by one you can end up with an infection and a fever.

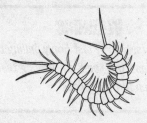

Ticks Ticks are very small. They crawl on to your body without you noticing them then burrow their way into your flesh, leaving their tail end sticking out. You usually discover them if you brush your hand against them or your clothing rubs against them. That's when you get a sharp stinging pain like a splinter. This is because the tick you have disturbed digs its way even deeper into your flesh. To get rid of ticks, pour alcohol on them to get them completely off their faces, then pull them out with tweezers.

Poison arrow tree frogs The skin of these frogs gives off one of the most deadly poisons known to mankind (but fortunately for them, not to tree frogs). No matter how enchanted you are by these brightly coloured little creatures, never be tempted to lick or snog them.

Some reassuring information:
Your hammock and your mosquito net are brilliant inventions which will protect you from masses of the stinging, buzzing, biting insect nuisances you meet in the jungle.

Some slightly worrying information:
Nevertheless, while you're hanging out in your hammock you must still watch out for the dreaded insects known as stinging fire ants. Some people call these ferocious

creatures 'the ants from hell'. Not content with just stinging, they also bite you! First, the fire ant sinks its powerful jaws into your flesh, then it repeatedly plunges in its stinger to inject its venom. Their stings burn intensely, then cause a blister which fills with pus. Some people go dizzy and start being sick when they've been stung by a fire ant and some even die. But most just end up with the amazingly irritating itch that follows the sting.

BEES, HORNETS AND WASPS

There are plenty of these noisy little buzzers in the jungle and they will all give you painful stings but, generally speaking, they aren't out to get you. Here's how to avoid trouble if you encounter a swarm:

1 Stay calm. Don't start waving your arms about and screaming like a hysterical soap star. This will give them the impression you're going to attack them. Then they will attack you and once a bee has stung you it sends a signal to its mates that it needs reinforcements, and then they'll all start on you.

Action-Seeker Tip

If a bee is annoyed it will often warn you off by bumping you with its head, not by stinging you. If this happens, don't swat it, just make a *beeline* for safety!

2 Avoid wearing flowery-patterned clothes. Bees and other insects might mistake you for an exotic rainforest plant! (Sorry, boys, but it's a fact.)

3 Keep your camp site tidy. Rotting food and mess will attract bees and wasps, not to mention lots of other nasty creatures such as rats, flies (and irate mothers).

If you're attacked by bees, wasps or hornets
DO cover your head if you can (maybe with your jacket or rucksack?).
DO run to safety. You should be able to outrun the bees – they can't fly faster than nine km/h.

DO run in a straight line. Don't dodge all over the place, as this will slow down your escape from the pursuing bees! DO get into anything that you can seal up securely so the bees can't get in, like a tent, sleeping bag (or an underground bank vault).

DON'T scream in terror. This will only make them more angry.

DON'T run towards other people because they will be attacked too (unless it's someone you think deserves a really good stinging).

DON'T hide under water. The bees will swarm above you and attack when you pop up for air.

DON'T rip off all your clothes, even if some of the bees have managed to get inside them. This will just give the bees more exposed flesh to sting (and also frighten the surrounding wildlife).

Coping with bee stings

If you do get stung by a bee, the faster you get the sting out the better. The sting has a pump attached to it that continues to squirt venom into the wound for one minute after you've been stung.

Action-Seeker Tip

If you get stung by a wasp, don't spend ages trying to pull out its stinger ... they don't leave them behind.

1 Remove the sting by pinching it between the nails of your thumb and forefinger or scraping it off with a knife blade or fingernail.

2 Don't forget those 'send-reinforcements' bee signals. So escape from Beeville as fast as you can.

3 If you've been stung on an arm or leg, lift it level with your heart to keep down the swelling. (Obviously, this could be quite tricky if you're stung on the leg and are busy running away from 10,000 furious bees but give it your best shot.)

4 Take an antihistamine tablet to reduce the swelling and itching. And put some antiseptic on the affected area if you can.

5 The swelling and redness may be worse the day after you've been stung. Don't worry, this is normal. However if the swelling is still painful and you've got a fever, you may have a secondary infection. In which case, you'll need to have it checked out at a hospital.

Action-Seeker Tip

If you get stung and haven't got any antiseptic with you, put some toothpaste on the swelling then douse it with cold water – this will soothe the pain and kill infection.

'African' bees

Some rather worrying information:

During the 1950s scientists were trying to create a super-bee that would make oodles of honey. Unfortunately, some of them escaped and mated with wild bees. The children they produced were ferocious (not to mention badly bee-hived). Many of these 'African' bees, as they became known, now live in the jungles of Central and South America and occasionally attack and kill humans, which is why they're also known as 'killer' bees. During your treks through the jungle, if you're really unlucky, you may bump into a swarm of African bees. If you do, it's probably a good thing if you know something about them:

● They look very similar to ordinary honey bees (because they *are* honey bees).

Honey bee   **Killer bee**   **Frisbee**

● There can be up to 60,000 killer bees in a swarm.
● If you go within a few dozen metres of their nests, they may begin swarming in order to defend them.
● Once their dander's up they will chase you for up to 300 metres and continue their attack for up to ten hours.
● A swarm of African bees looks like a small dark cloud and sounds like a giant electric food whisk.

HAVE YOU BEEN PAYING ATTENTION?

1 If a mosquito lands on you, immediately ...
a) head butt it.
b) squidge it.
c) eat it.

2 Mosquitoes breed in ...
a) honeymoon hotels.
b) swampy areas.
c) a hurry.

3 A leech is a sort of ...
a) fruit, also known as the Chinese gooseberry.
b) worm.
c) door fastener.

4 The best way to avoid being stung by bees or wasps is to ...
a) cover yourself in raspberry jam.
b) wear a black-and-yellow striped jump suit.
c) remain calm.

DEALING WITH SNAKES

Lots of people imagine the jungle to be one slithering great mass of poisonous snakes. It isn't. There are lots of snakes in the world's jungles but they keep themselves to themselves. Most jungle visitors hardly ever see a snake, never mind get bitten by one. But sensible action-seekers should take precautions and find out a bit about these fascinating reptiles before setting off, just in case.

Some things you should know about snakes
● Snakes are deaf, so you might well surprise one that's sunbathing or sleeping on the track.
● Snakes are unable to close their eyes. This means you can't tell if they're asleep or not.
● Snakes are sometimes attracted to warm sleeping human bodies and have been known to snuggle up to action-seekers in their sleeping bags. So keep well zipped up.

The really dangerous jungle snake file

Jumping vipers
Where to watch out for jumping vipers: Jungles in Southern Mexico, Honduras, Guatemala, Costa Rica, Panama and El Salvador.
What they look like: They grow to between 60 and 120 cm in length. They have thick bodies and their colour varies from brown to grey with dark blotches on their back.

How they behave: During the daytime they often hide under large logs and piles of leaves and are really difficult to spot. They come out in the early evening to feed on lizards, rats, mice and frogs (and action-seekers).

Worrying fact: When they strike at you they actually leap right off the ground.

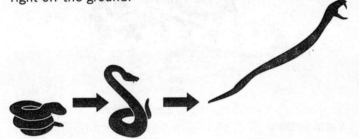

Bushmasters

Where to watch out for bushmasters: The jungles of Nicaragua, Costa Rica, Panama, Trinidad and Brazil.

What they look like: They're big! They grow to anywhere between 2 metres and 3.7 metres in length, and their fangs can measure up to nearly 4 cm. They're a pale brown or pinkish colour with dark brown or black blotches on them. Their scales are really rough (and so are they).

How they behave: They live in the deepest jungle and usually feed at night.

A worrying fact: If you get bitten by a bushmaster, you're in big trouble.

Another worrying fact: If you don't get medical attention immediately you usually die from the bite.

Yet another worrying fact: You're most likely to get bitten by a bushmaster in jungles that are many days' travel away from medical help.

Coral snakes

Where to watch out for coral snakes: The jungles and swamps of Central and South America. Sometimes you may find them in jungle villages too.

What they look like: They're between 60 cm and 115 cm long and are really beautiful with black, red and yellow markings. Their short fangs are always fixed in the erect position.

Action-Seeker Tip

Some other, less dangerous snakes have similar markings. However, you can identify coral snakes because their red markings are always next to their yellow ones whereas on the harmless lookalikes the red bands are always separated from the yellow ones by black bands.

How they behave: Coral snakes are really shy.

A worrying fact: When a coral snake bites you it chews you so that its venom works its way into the wound.

Another worrying fact: The venom of the coral snake will make you suffocate to death after you've been bitten.

Eyelash pit vipers

Where to watch out for eyelash pit vipers: The jungles of Southern Mexico, Central America, Colombia, Ecuador and Venezuela.

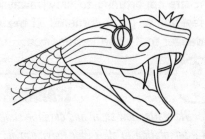

What they look like: They can be anywhere between 45 cm and 75 cm in length. They've got several spiny scales over each eye (like eyelashes). Some are bright yellow all over and some are covered in reddish-yellow spots.

How they behave: They live in low-hanging branches of trees and hardly ever come down to the ground.

A worrying fact: Eyelash pit vipers are really bad-tempered and will attack you for no reason at all.

Another worrying fact: Because they hang about in low-hanging branches they're most likely to bite you on your face or neck!

Yet another worrying fact: The bite causes really bad damage to your flesh tissue and people often die after being bitten by them.

Avoiding snakes

1 Always walk carefully and watch where you're stepping.

2 If you do happen to meet a snake on the track, give it the opportunity to crawl away rather than making it feel you've got it cornered. If the snake thinks you are a danger to it, it will attack you.

WARNING

No matter how small and cute the snake may appear, resist the temptation to click your tongue at it, stroke it or try to make friends with it.

3 If you come across a log in the track, step on to it rather than over it. When you're on top of it, check the track in front of you before moving on. Snakes are very fond of lying around near logs. (It makes them feel superior and sophisticated.)

Worrying fact: A snake can strike over a distance of half its length. So if it's two metres long and you're one metre away from it, it can reach you in just one strike.

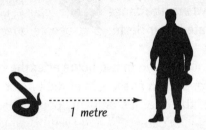

1 metre

4 If you need to move a stone or a log, do it with a stick rather than your hands.

5 Always wear something on your feet that will protect them from a snakebite – preferably thick boots.

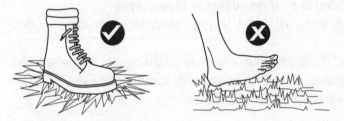

Treating a snakebite

Before treating a snakebite, find out whether the snake was poisonous or not by doing the following checks:

1 If you've been bitten by a snake that isn't poisonous you'll see rows of teeth marks in your skin where it bit you.

2 If you have been bitten by a poisonous snake you will have puncture marks too. That's where the fangs have penetrated your flesh.

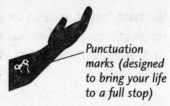

Punctuation marks (designed to bring your life to a full stop)

3 A few minutes or up to two hours after the bite: If you get a nosebleed, pain at the site of the bite or a swelling at the site of the bite, it's probably poisonous.

4 Between one and a half to two hours after the bite: If you have difficulty breathing, feel weak, begin twitching, can't move your legs or arms, or go numb, this also means the bite is poisonous.

What to do if the snakebite is poisonous

1 Keep calm. Tell yourself everything's going to be OK.

2 Take off your watch or any rings or bracelets you might be wearing (along with anything else you wouldn't want to be seen dead in).

3 Make sure you can breathe properly, especially if you've been bitten near your face or neck.

4 Clean the area of skin where you've been bitten.

5 Try not to move the injured area. If you decide to go for help, *don't* run.

6 Apply a tourniquet. This means tying a bootlace or some strips of cloth tightly above the wound to stop the snakebite poison from travelling further into the bloodstream.

7 Keep the infected area around the bite cool and dry.

8 If you have any anti-snakebite serum with you, take it as directed on the bottle.

9 Get medical help as soon as you can. This may involve signalling for help (see page 49).

DEALING WITH CROCODILES

You're travelling along a jungle river in a small canoe when, reaching for your camera, you lose your balance and capsize the boat. After a few panicky moments in the water, you manage to grasp your overturned craft and begin to swim towards the river bank, pulling it behind you. But as you do, you notice what appear to be several long, greenish-brown 'logs' lying in the mud at the water's edge. A moment later, one of these 'logs' gets up, waddles across the mud, then slides into the main river and begins swimming towards you. At this point your heart begins to pound wildly against your ribs. You've suddenly realized that this is not a log, but a huge crocodile! Frozen with fear, you stop swimming and begin to tread water, watching in terror as the monstrous creature gets nearer and nearer and nearer. Questions flash through your mind: Should you remain in the water and try to out-swim the monster? Or head for the opposite bank and try to outrun it? And if the worst does happen and it does get hold of you ... what then? But you must make up your mind soon. It's almost upon you!

Escaping from a crocodile

You might want to try out-swimming the croc for starters. Crocodiles are powerful, but not particularly fast, swimmers. Over a short distance you'll probably be able to get away from it by using the crawl stroke (or by attaching a small outboard motor to your bottom). However, don't make a habit of challenging crocs to swimming races. If you do decide to head for land, don't think you're going to be safe there. Crocs are really fast runners.

If the croc manages to catch you, you've got a slightly more challenging sort of situation to deal with. Once a croc has got hold of you in the water it rolls over and over. This action is known as the 'Death Roll' and the idea behind it is to make you become totally disoriented so you don't know whether you're coming or going (though chances are you're *definitely* going!). Here's what to do if the worst does come to the worst, whether you're in the water or on land:

1 Cover the creature's eyes. This will calm it down.

2 Attack its eyes and nose with your fist or a weapon, e.g. a stick, machete (or atom bomb).

3 Make its jaws open by punching it on the nose.

4 Try to stop the croc shaking you in its jaws by clamping its mouth shut (or asking it if it's ever considered turning vegetarian).

Serving suggestion

If you do happen to win your scrap with the croc, why not have it for lunch? Crocodile flesh is edible and is said to taste like chicken (some chicken!).

More nasties to beware of when you're around water

If you can, avoid splashing across isolated pools and sluggish water. These are the sort of places where electric eels, anaconda snakes and leeches live. And take care when you're crossing pools and rivers with sandy bottoms. They're favourite places for stingrays to hang out. Slap the water with the flat of your hand to scare them away.

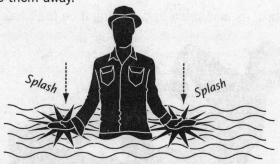

Splash

Splash

If you're swimming in pools or rivers, wear something on your feet. Crabs and turtles can nip off your toes!

Take extra care when you're wading through shallow pools. There may be piranha fish in them, particularly if it's the dry season. The piranhas get stranded in the pools when the river goes down. As oxygen and food get scarce, the piranhas become increasingly aggressive and, as a result, they often go into a feeding frenzy and use their razor sharp teeth to attack anything that moves, i.e. your feet and legs.

Jungle tale

A farmer was leading a donkey across a shallow jungle river when the long rope it was tied to suddenly begun to twitch and jerk violently. He turned to see the donkey thrashing around in the water and screaming in terror. Attached to it were hundreds of piranha fish which were busily eating it alive. Within minutes, all that was left of the poor animal was its skeleton. Just before it began the crossing a thorn had cut the donkey's flesh and the moment it entered the water the piranhas smelled the blood from the wound and went into a feeding frenzy.

HAVE YOU BEEN PAYING ATTENTION?

1 Snakes are deaf so ...
a) always speak to them very slowly and in a clear voice.
b) you might well surprise one that's sunbathing or sleeping on the track.
c) don't be surprised to see them using sign language.

2 If you come across a log in the track ...
a) talk to it quietly and calmly.
b) make a note of it in your log book.
c) step on it rather than over it.

3 If a snake bites you, you must ...
a) report it to the RSPCA (Royal Society for the Prevention of Cruelty to Action-seekers).
b) tie it in a triple reef knot.
c) remain calm.

4 When a crocodile rolls over with you in its jaws it's known as ...
a) the sausage roll.
b) a somewhat distressing experience.
c) the Death Roll.

5 Eyelash pit vipers ...
a) live down coal mines.
b) wear false eyelashes.
c) are really aggressive.

Conclusion

Congratulations, action-seeker! You've taken the first giant step towards becoming a fully-fledged jungle explorer. All you have to do now is decide how you're going to put your new-found knowledge to the test. A white-knuckle rafting trip down the Amazon? An awesome gorilla-watching trek in central Africa? A thrilling elephant-back journey through the jungles of northern Thailand? The choices are endless.

However, no matter which terrific jungle experience you go for, one thing's for sure: as you get to grips with the heart-stopping and thrilling challenges the jungle will throw at you, you will discover deep inside yourself, reserves of courage, resourcefulness, intelligence and mental toughness you never even knew you had.

Soon, as your senses sharpen, your survival skills develop and your confidence grows, the jungle will begin to feel like a second home to you. And then experiences that would no doubt terrify those less adventurous than yourself, such as encounters with giant anacondas or brushes with bird-eating spiders, will bother you less than a lost bus pass or a seriously tricky spelling test.

And, once your jungle skills have become as natural and automatic as finding your way around your local supermarket or buying a pair of trainers, all sorts of opportunities await you. You might become a jungle guide, leading parties of awestruck and admiring tourists into the rainforest, showing them natural wonders that only you know where to find, and confident in the knowledge that whatever emergency arises they will be safe in your capable hands. Or a film-maker, producing breathtaking jungle wildlife movies to be shown all over the world. Or an eco-warrior, using your rainforest knowledge to outwit the business moguls who are determined to turn the world's jungles into warehouses full of flat-pack furniture. Or you might become the sort of intrepid and fearless individual who leads parties of rescuers to seek out lost trekkers or aircrash victims. Action-seeker, all sorts of exciting experiences are out there for you!

And should you find that a trip to one of the world's rainforests is slightly beyond your weekly pocket money, you could always test out your survival skills in your local park or woods, or even in your own back garden. (But if you do, watch out for those killer squirrels and terrifying, 2-cm-long earthworms!).

So, globe-trotter ... zip off to where it's hotter! Then hitch up your backpack and hit that jungle track! What are you waiting for? Go explore!

Glossary

There are lots of words you'll use as a jungle explorer that are special to the thrilling world of rainforests and wilderness survival. Here are some of them:

acclimatize get used to a new climate or environment

backpack/rucksack a bag carried on the back by hikers and campers

bow drill device for making fire, using a string bow and a sharp stick

compass an instrument used to find directions

dehydration serious loss of body fluid, usually by sweating and not drinking enough

disorientated to become confused about directions

hammock cloth or netting hung by its ends and used for sleeping in (and falling out of)

larva young animal, usually an insect that's really different looking from its adult version, e.g. a caterpillar

machete a heavy knife used as a tool in South America

malaria tropical swamp fever transmitted by mosquitoes

mangrove type of tree that grows in coastal tropical swamps

Morse code signalling system in which each letter is represented by a series of dots and dashes, long and short light flashes or sound signals

orang-utan a reddish-brown ape which lives in the jungles of Sumatra and Borneo (and zoos all over the world)

primary jungle jungle that's been there for absolutely yonks (but is really looking forward to going to big school)

rainforest another word for the jungle

ridge pole piece of wood forming the ridge of a roof on a shelter

secondary jungle jungle that's grown back after primary jungle has been cut down and cultivated (and is tremendously difficult to walk through)

solar still a device for using the sun's heat to get moisture from plants

tepee conical frame shelter of leaning poles, normally covered by an animal skin

termites fat, pasty-looking creepy-crawlies sometimes referred to as white ants

vine woody plants that put out long shoots which climb other plants and trees

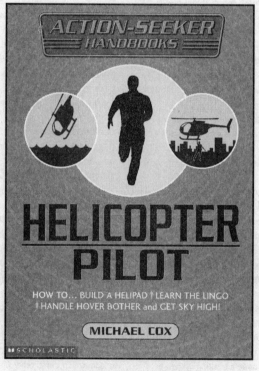